JOHN POWI

The SECRET of Staying in Love

Loving Relationships through Communication

TABOR
PUBLISHING

Allen, Texas

Photo Credits

Tom Bean/The Stock Market   68
Jean-Claude Lejeune   21, 26, 35, 41, 45, 55, 72, 87, 113, 128, 151, 159

Cover design: Karen Malzeke-McDonald

Calligraphy: Bob Niles

Send all inquiries to:
Tabor Publishing
One DLM Park
Allen, Texas 75002

Library of Congress Catalog Card Number 74-84712

Printed in the United States of America

ISBN 1-55924-280-9

2   3   4   5   94   93   92   91

This book is gratefully dedicated to

Bernice Brady.

Bee has been a great source of support in many of my previous attempts to write. She has generously contributed an excellent critical eye, a cultivated literary sense, and especially a confident kind of encouragement. She was unequalled as a proofreader.

She did not help with the preparation of this book. On June 11, 1973, Bee received a "better offer." She was called by the Author and Lord of the Universe to join the celebration at the banquet of eternal life.

Even in your absence, you were present, Bee. This one is gratefully dedicated to you.

Acknowledgments

Excerpt from *Man's Search for Meaning* by Viktor Frankl. Beacon Press, Boston.

Excerpt from *Modern Man in Search of a Soul* by C. G. Jung. Harcourt Brace Jovanovich, New York.

Excerpts from *The Art of Loving* by Erich Fromm, Vol. 9 in *World Perspectives*. Edited by Ruth Nanda Anshen. Copyright © 1956 by Erich Fromm. By permission of Harper & Row. These excerpts also reprinted with the permission of George Allen & Unwin, Ltd., London.

Excerpt from *Escape from Freedom* by Erich Fromm. Holt, Rinehart & Winston, New York.

Excerpt from *Markings* by Dag Hammarskjold translated by Lief Sjoberg and W. H. Auden. Copyright © 1964 by Alfred A. Knopf, Inc. and Faber & Faber, Ltd. Reprinted by permission of Alfred A. Knopf, Inc. This excerpt also reprinted with the permission of Faber & Faber, Ltd., London.

Excerpt from *Conceptions of Modern Psychiatry* by Dr. Harry Stack Sullivan. W. W. Norton & Co., Inc., New York.

Excerpts reprinted from *Letters to a Young Poet* by Rainer Maria Rilke, translation by M. D. Herter Norton. By permission of W. W. Norton & Company, Inc. Copyright 1934 and 1954 by W. W. Norton & Company, Inc. Copyright renewed 1962 by M. D. Herter Norton. These excerpts also reprinted with the permission of the Hogarth Press, Ltd., London.

Excerpt from *The Miracle of Dialogue* by Reuel Howe. Seabury Press, New York.

Contents

Be patient toward all that is unsolved
in your heart. . . .
Try to love the questions themselves. . . .

Do not now seek the answers,
which cannot be given
because you would not be able
to live them.
And the point is,
to live everything.

Live the questions now.
Perhaps you will then
gradually,
without noticing it,
Live along some distant day
into the answers.

Rainer Maria Rilke

The human condition: needs, options, addictions

My sisters and brothers
in our human family:

I am writing again because I think I have something to say to you. Perhaps you have read something which I have written previously. It is not important, really. What I wrote then reflected where I was then as a person. This book is to share with you where I have gone from that point, where I am now. What I really want to say to you is that I think I have lived along into some new insights and answers. Now I want to share them with you, and to have your reaction to them. There are, of course, many questions about the mystery of me, the mystery of you, and the mystery of our relationship which are still unsolved in my heart. There are so many questions which I must continue to love because I am as yet unable to live their answers.

In the periods of waiting for answers, we can feel very small and helpless. We can feel dominated and intimidated by the "professionals" who have the necessary degrees and "credentials" to instruct us. I would like to assure you that I do not come as one of these. I do not come as a teacher but as a brother. I hold out my offering, the offering of myself, in trembling, uncertain hands. Whatever is helpful, please keep as yours. Let whatever is not helpful sift and slip softly through your fingers.

Human Needs

I am convinced that we were meant to live at peace within ourselves, filled with a deep joy. I am convinced that there should be going on in the heart of each of us not a funeral but a celebration of life and love. Prophets of gloom, with their "valley of tears" mentality and vocabulary, have always sounded unreal to me. With good old Saint Irenaeus of the second century I have always believed that "the glory of God is a person who is fully alive!" Of course, there is no problemless Camelot or painless Utopia. The tension resulting from problems and pain is part of the whole piece. It usually directs our attention to a growing edge of life, a territory for expansion. For myself, I do not regret the problems or pain in my past life, but only the apathy, the moments when I was not "fully alive."

The essential sadness of our human family is that very few of us even approach the realization of our full potential. I accept the estimate of the theoreticians that average human beings accomplish only 10 percent of their promise. They see only 10 percent of the beauty in the world about them. They hear only 10 percent of the music and poetry in the universe. They smell only a tenth of the world's fragrance, and taste only a tenth of the deliciousness of being alive. They are only 10 percent open to their emotions, to tenderness, to wonder and awe. Their minds embrace only a small part of the thoughts, reflections, and understanding of which they are capable. Their hearts are only 10 percent alive with love. They will die without ever having really lived or really loved. To me this is the most frightening of all possibilities. I would really hate to think that you or I might die without having really lived and really loved.

The Sadness of Failure

If we were made to be fully alive, why do we so often find ourselves reduced to making the best of a bad thing? Obviously, in our lives and in the lives of so many others, something needed for the fullness of life is missing or at least is not being recognized and enjoyed. Somehow, somewhere, something has gone wrong. Somewhere along the way the light has failed. In his verse "Out of Order," André Auw describes his reactions when he comes upon the scene of a young mother trying to explain to her four-year-old boy that the popcorn machine cannot give out its contents:

> *"You can't get any popcorn, Child. The*
> *machine is out of order. See, there*
> *is a sign on the machine."*

> *But he didn't understand. After all, he had the*
> *desire, and he had the money, and he*
> *could see the popcorn in the machine.*
> *And yet somehow, somewhere, something*
> *was wrong because he couldn't get the*
> *popcorn.*

> *The boy walked back with his mother, and he*
> *wanted to cry.*

> *And Lord, I too felt like weeping, weeping for*
> *people who have become locked-in,*
> *jammed, broken machines filled with*
> *goodness that other people need and*
> *want and yet will never come to enjoy,*
> *because somehow, somewhere,*
> *something has gone wrong inside.*

All forms of life have optimum conditions and essential requirements for health, growth, the fullness of life. When the environment of each being furnishes these conditions and requirements, the fullness of life is possible, the potential riches can be realized. When people are fully alive, saying a vibrant *yes* to the full human experience and a full-hearted *amen* to love, there is an indication that their human needs are being met. But when the contrary is true, when discomfort, frustration, and crippling emotions take over in a human life, there is a contraindication that the human needs of these people are not being met. It may be through their own failure or through the failure of those closest to them, but they are just not getting what they need. Somehow, somewhere, something has gone wrong in those lives. Starvation and disintegration have set in.

The Fundamental Human Need

Human beings are not simple. They are composites of body, mind, and spirit, and they have needs on all three levels of their existence. They have needs and appetites that are physical, psychological, and spiritual. Frustration at any one of these levels can produce agony in the whole organism.

However, there is a growing consensus of opinion that there is one need so fundamental and so essential that if it is met, everything else will almost certainly harmonize in a general sense of well-being. When this need is properly nourished, the whole human organism will be healthy and the person will be happy. This need is a *true and deep love of self, a genuine and joyful self-acceptance, an authentic self-esteem,* which result in *an interior sense of celebration:* "It's good to be me . . . I am very happy to be me!"

Did something in you become immediately uncomfortable and uneasy when you read the previous statement? Conditioned as we are by our culture, we seem to be emotionally allergic to the very vocabulary of love of self. The thought of rejoicing in and celebrating our own unique goodness seems like a very distant and alien thought. Immediate associations of egotism, vanity, and selfishness rush like dark clouds into our minds. I suspect that most of us never get through the crust of this difficult vocabulary and these suspicions to find the most important reality of any human life and the beginning of all human love.

Sometimes I wonder if it is the reality of self-love and self-appreciation that threatens us as much as the anticipated reaction of others. We might think that others would reject us if self-esteem ever floated to the surface of our communications. As an experiment with our societal attitude toward self-acceptance, I once introduced myself to my university class, on our first day together, as someone who really accepted, believed in, and loved himself. I told them that I was a very good person, kind, generous, and loving. I assured them of my adequate intelligence, and of my instinctual feeling that I am a good teacher with a stimulating message. I tried to do this in a sincere, factual, and honest manner.

Some of my students laughed nervously, wondering if I could possibly be serious, while others fixed me with a stare that wondered: Should we shoot him or spray him? One girl, who appeared to be on the verge of nausea, turned to the person sitting next to her and announced not too silently: "Yuk! What conceit!" After this extended self-introduction as the kind of teacher you always wanted but were afraid to expect, I began to present the material of the course. Only in the following class period did I explain my experiment to the students. (Even to this day I have never been fully sure that all of them believed the explanation.) Anyway, I invited them to relisten to their emotional reactions to my self-

introduction. "Were you happy that I could openly acknowledge and publicly admit my self-appreciation? Were you able
to join me in my celebration of being me? Or did you feel
resentment, suspicion?" I tried to convince my students that
their reactions were telling them something about themselves, about our society, and about how we react to
expressed love of self.

In his book *Escape from Freedom,* Erich Fromm insists that
the egotism, vanity, and conceit which we are constantly
suspecting in one another are really the very opposite of true
self-love, self-acceptance, and self-celebration.

> Selfishness is not identical with self-love but its very
> opposite. Selfishness is one kind of greediness. Like
> all greediness, it contains an insatiability, as a
> consequence of which there is never any real
> satisfaction. Greed is a bottomless pit which exhausts
> the person in an endless effort to satisfy the need
> without ever reaching satisfaction. . . . The selfish
> person is always anxiously concerned with himself;
> he is never satisfied, is always restless, always driven
> by the fear of not getting enough, of missing
> something, of being deprived of something. He is filled
> with burning envy of anyone who might have more.
> . . . This type of person is basically not fond of himself
> at all, but deeply dislikes himself. . . . Selfishness is
> rooted in this very lack of fondness of oneself. . . .
> Narcissism, like selfishness, is an overcompensation
> for the basic lack of self-love. . . . He loves neither
> others nor himself.

We have here a question that each of us must silently,
reflectively consider. What are my true feelings? When I hear
something complimentary about another, why do I say: "Don't
tell him. It might go to his head"? Why do I not want others

to be happy with themselves? I don't want "it" to go to his head. What is "it" that I don't want in the head of my brother or sister? What *do* I want in his or her head? If another rejoices in some success, why do I immediately accuse that person of bragging? Why have I become such a jealous guardian of his or her humility? Why does it concern me so much?

Perhaps the answer to these and similar questions will lead me to the realization that I do not want others to love themselves because I am unable to love myself. It is a psychological truism that our attitudes toward others are conditioned by our fundamental attitudes toward ourselves. If I cannot openly and honestly acknowledge my own strengths and assets, I will not want others to acknowledge theirs. You and I must sit for a while and ponder this question, because the answer could be seriously crippling or slowly destroying us. Everything depends upon and flows from our openness to ourselves. When we lose the ability to appreciate ourselves and enjoy being ourselves, all sorts of dark and painful things rush in to fill the void.

> As you ramble through life, my Brother,
> Whatever be your goal,
> Keep your eye upon the doughnut,
> And not upon the hole.

Bertrand Russell once said, "A man cannot possibly be at peace with others until he has learned to be at peace with himself." Rabbi Joshua Liebman has advocated a rewording of the biblical command of love so that it will read: "Love and believe in yourself properly and you will love and believe in your neighbor." A psychiatrist-spokesperson for the Payne-Whitney Psychiatric Clinic in New York has been quoted as saying: "If people had a healthy love of themselves instead of hating themselves and feeling bad, if only they would love the child in themselves instead of despising the weakness, our case load would be cut in half."

Most contemporary psychotherapy, as typified in the current enthusiasm for Transactional Analysis and its central goal of learning to feel Okay, is designed to help people toward one thing: to help them adopt a kindly, positive, and accepting attitude toward themselves. Most people are very far from this, even though we could easily be deceived by surface attitudes. From a literal reading of these surface attitudes, we might wrongly conclude that most people really do love themselves. On the surface, most of us accuse and attack others while justifying ourselves. However, deep down in areas that we are normally afraid to confront and explore, the exact opposite is true. We give others a probation or suspended sentence while we "throw the book at" ourselves. A psychiatrist at the Mental Health Clinic of the University of South Carolina medical school has said: "Our biggest job is to help patients find out what is good about themselves. It never fails: as they begin to like themselves a little better, they begin simultaneously to get well."

Dr. Robert H. Felix, a former director of the National Institute for Mental Health, describes this healthy love and acceptance of self as a "feeling of dignity, of belonging, a feeling of worthwhileness, a feeling of adequacy." Dr. Felix continues: "We must learn to regard ourselves with understanding. I must learn to enjoy being myself. I would not want to be anyone else. I would want to be only myself."

There is no doubt in my mind that a deep understanding of and a serious effort to achieve true love of self is the beginning of all human growth and happiness. In an effort to establish this as fact, I would here like to quote the great psychiatrist Carl G. Jung, from his book *Modern Man in Search of a Soul:*

Perhaps this sounds very simple, but simple things are always the most difficult. In actual life it requires the greatest discipline to be simple, and the acceptance of self is the essence of the moral problem and the epitome of a whole outlook upon life. That I feed the hungry, that I forgive an insult, that I love my enemy in the name of Christ—all these are undoubtedly great virtues. What I do unto the least of my brethren, that I do unto Christ. But what if I should discover that the least amongst them all, the poorest of all the beggars, the most impudent of all the offenders, the very enemy himself—that these are within me, and that I myself stand in need of the alms of my own kindness—that I myself am the enemy who must be loved—what then? . . . Neurosis is an inner cleavage—the state of being at war with oneself. Everything that accentuates this cleavage makes the patient worse, and everything that mitigates it tends to heal the patient.

The very thing that I am so reluctant to concede to others and to myself is, in fact, our greatest need: true love and appreciation of self. Self-doubt and self-hatred are the common cancers that have so badly ravaged humanity, distorting and destroying social relationships and trust. I am sure that almost all human neuroses and moral evils stem from this one common cause: the absence of true love of oneself.

The Origin of Our Problems

Of course, it all begins in those most important years of any human life, the first two. A baby is born into this world like a living question searching for answers. Who am I? What am I worth? What is life about? What am I supposed to be and do?

The answers start coming in immediately. If a child receives an abundance of affection, hugs, kisses, lullabies, laughing and warmth, the answers will be optimistic and joyful. They will seep in and be indelibly recorded. The child will begin to know the one thing she or he needs most to know: I am lovable! I don't have to do anything or be anything but myself. I am valuable and worthwhile in myself.

However, if the parents are unable or unwilling to express affection, if they are cold and matter-of-fact, irritated by the baby's middle-of-the-night needs or impatient with incontinence, the infant will absorb these facts. The nonverbal communication of this irritation, displeasure, or even anger is recorded forever in the human organism of the child. Somehow the baby senses that he or she has caused these reactions. The child is not only recording these messages but is also recording the personal emotional responses of doubt, anxiety, and insecurity. They will play back to and in the child for the rest of his or her life.

Later, when the baby begins to talk and listen, those impressions of self and personal worth will be deepened through verbal communication. If the baby hears warm words, like "I love you . . . My Darling . . . Good boy [girl] . . ." the child will feel good and lovable. The child will begin to develop a sense of personal worth and security that will dispose him or her to a lifetime of openness and friendliness with others. The child will always anticipate warmth and love from others, and so be inclined to trust them and be open with them.

Most of us, to a greater or lesser degree, have heard a very different message. We were offered love, but it was always somehow "conditional" love. Babies, even in their first encounters with words, can easily hear conditions attached to their parents' love: "If you are quiet . . . If you eat your

dinner . . . If you don't make a mess . . . If you act like your
brother or sister . . ." Later, as children develop so do these
conditions of tentative love evolve. Growing children hear a
new set of stipulations for receiving love: "If you help around
the house . . . If you stay clean . . . If you get good grades in
school . . ." The point is always clear whatever the conditions
may be. There is a "price of admission" for love, and you've
got to pay it. Your worth is not in yourself, but in something
else, in your appearance, your actions, your success, in being
and doing what is expected of you.

Many parents tend to use this kind of manipulation by the
pulling and pushing of various levers: smiles or frowns,
warmth or coldness, words or silence. Today we would call
it "behavior modification." The desired behavior is achieved
by providing rewards for compliance and penalties for failure.
The price that such treatment exacts of children can be
catastrophic in terms of their self-image and self-love. Children
who have been taught their lessons by having love turned on
and off eventually conclude that their sole worth and
goodness lie in their ability to fulfill the needs and wishes of
others. In no sense do they live *for themselves* but only *for
others.*

The usual demands made by conditional, parental love are
compliance, cooperation, and conformity. Children are
coerced into being like somebody else, doing their best
always, being a success, working hard, causing no trouble,
glorifying the family name, making their parents proud, and
so on. Of course, when all the conditions are added up, they
are just too much. Under conditions like these, children can
only fail, and in failure be deprived of love. After all, failure
means that you didn't pay the necessary price of admission
to love. This, of course, leads to self-hatred, whether
consciously admitted or not. And this self-hatred is the

beginning of a sad and self-destructive life. Erich Fromm, in his *Art of Loving,* writes:

> To be loved because of one's merit, because one
> deserves it, always leaves doubt; maybe I did not please
> the person whom I want to love me, maybe this or
> that—there is always a fear that love could disappear.
> Furthermore, "deserved" love easily leaves a bitter
> feeling that one is not loved for oneself, that one is
> loved only because one pleases, that one is, in the last
> analysis, not loved at all but used.

Adjustments to the Painful Reality

The human organism is extremely resourceful in adjusting to various situations. It has a way of compensating for losses and attempting recovery. To the extent that infants or children have not been assured of their worth and lovability, they begin to adapt, to act and react in ways that will spare them the sharpest edge of pain or fill in their painful voids. Some of their devices will be designed to avoid further pain, while others will be directed to inviting and winning love. I would like to run through a brief and partial list of such devices, behavioral symptoms that appear in people who have not learned to love and esteem themselves. The severity of the symptom, the extent to which the device is employed, will always be proportionate to the greater or lesser absence of true self-love and self-esteem.

Exaggerating or Bragging. By definition bragging here implies self-flattery with the intended purpose of achieving recognition and a sense of worth, both in one's own eyes and the eyes of others. As we often sense, braggarts are not only trying to convince us of their ability or worth, but also themselves. In general they are met with unkindness. Many people volunteer for the work of putting braggarts in their place. It is a sad reversal, because braggarts are convinced that love and recognition are conditional, and they are trying to present their credentials as the price of admission.

A Critical Attitude. People who do not love themselves may adapt to their condition by becoming critical of others, always finding and pointing out their faults. Of course, such accusations are really self-accusations, though they do not realize this. Their criticism is based on a projection of what they think of themselves. Since hating themselves for their worthlessness and faults would be too painful, they project their faults into others, and proceed to ventilate their venom with deadly aim.

Rationalization. People without love of self have no sense of personal worth, and their only assumed worth rests on their ability to perform. Consequently, when their perform-ance leaves something to be desired, they immediately excuse themselves, and rationalize their failure. To admit that they are wrong, to confess their faults and failures would involve too much pain. They can never afford to lose an argument or have false information. Their worth is only conditional, and such failures would destroy the last vestiges of self-respect.

Perfectionism. Some people are driven to accomplish whatever they attempt with meticulous perfection. With such perfectionists, performance is the assumed condition for recognition and love; so their performance becomes crucially important. They are always trying to pass the test, pay the price of admission admitting them to feelings of personal worth. Measuring up to the expectations of those who can give recognition or refuse it becomes their treadmill.

Shyness. Since shy people have been taught that others will accept them only on certain conditions, their basic reaction to people is fear. They fear others' criticism, evaluation, and, in the end, rejection. To avoid running this risk, they may wall themselves in, protect themselves by wearing a veil of shyness. At least in certain situations in which they cannot be confident, they feel very shy and withdrawn. Shyness is a kind of psychological insulation against failure, and it is a serious matter since it is their person and their worth that are always on trial.

Self-depreciation. One way of adjusting to this painful condition of emptiness is to paint such a depressing picture of oneself that others will not expect much. They will refrain from criticism, and maybe even extend some sympathy. The portrait of the "deprived victim" will not threaten us, and so our treatment of such victims may even include an attempt to build them up.

Anger. People afflicted by a sense of personal worthlessness first hate their own inadequacy and futility. Soon they are hating themselves. When this anger is turned in on themselves, it takes the form of depression and despondency. It somehow lessens the pain to ventilate anger on others. In fact, angry people may be acting out in some temper tantrum their own very painful condition.

Defensive Docility. Another possible adjustment to the absence of true self-esteem is to become a submissive observer of every regulation, law, and rule with mechanical precision. The people in question have learned very early in life that such compliance brings a reward, a smile or embrace, so they keep trying. They attempt to be completely good and obedient. They feel safer from criticism this way, since they can hide their real self behind rules and their observance of them. They are continually angling for approval, striving for security.

Becoming a Loner. Obviously, some people reason, it is safer not to get involved with others. Other people will only find out that they are not lovable in themselves. Others will start imposing all the same old, tiring conditions for recognition and love. It's easier just to avoid this exhausting game, to go it alone. These wounded spirits may play at surface sociability, but deep down they are still and choose to remain essentially alone.

Overachieving. To some extent we all believe that what we *do* will make up for what we fail to *be* in ourselves. We overachievers are tempted to want the achievement of "great deeds." We want to own big and magnificent things, in the hopes that these will get us attention and recognition. To many people caught up in this intended adjustment, achievements and possessions are construed as an extension of self, and such people need all the extensions they can get.

Masks, Roles, Facades. People who have received and know only conditional love cannot endure much criticism of their actions, opinions, or person. They have been hurt and want to risk no further vulnerability. Criticism of their actions or person would undermine their whole existence. So they may seek immunity from such devastating criticism by putting some kind of an act on the stage rather than by putting themselves on the line. If people criticize their act, they can always change it. If people criticize their honest person or authentic acts, they would feel destroyed.

Introjection. Basically dissatisfied with themselves, people who feel worthless will tend to identify with someone else, preferably a public or private hero. They will be like a little boy taking on the mannerisms of an athletic star or a little girl pretending she is a favorite television character. Both "introject" qualities and abilities they do not have. Even this charade is consoling.

Absolute Agreeability. One of the saddest adjustments made by people who cannot love themselves is to play at being the all-time nice person. Such people will offer their agreement on any subject at any time in order to barter for a little recognition and approval. They are not really genuine. They are sad and compromising. However, they would rather settle for absolute agreeability than the alternative of absolute loneliness.

Cynicism, Suspicion. Because cynics perceive little value in themselves, they also have little trust in themselves. In the blind belief that everyone else is really like them, they extend and project their own self-distrust. They believe in and trust no one.

Timidity. Unlike shyness, which concerns reluctance with respect to personal relationships, timidity refers to a reluctance to venture, to undertake new projects. Afraid to love and afraid to be loved because of the danger of ultimate failure and rejection, people without a sense of personal worth will be afraid to attempt anything of significance. They are, in fact, cut off from much of reality by their fears. They will not try the new because they might be wrong. They are afraid to express themselves because they might make a mistake or someone might challenge them. They fear making overtures to others because they might be disliked.

Summary

Everyone is born with unique and unconditional value. Each of us is mysterious and unrepeatable in the whole course of human history, made after the image and likeness of God. But we can know ourselves only as we are reflected in the eyes of others. Consequently, our basic endowment of self-appreciation is largely the gift of our parents. However, most of us—and I think all of us to some extent—have perceived that their love for us was only conditional, that it was turned on only when we met their conditions and turned off when we failed to meet them. We concluded that their love was not based on what we are but was conditioned on our performance. So we came to think that our value is somehow outside ourselves. There is no cause within for true self-love, self-esteem, self-appreciation. There is no occasion for celebration.

When worthiness of love becomes a matter of passing tests and fulfilling conditions, we begin to experience more failure than success. In the experience of repeated failure, there is conflict, fear, frustration, pain, and ultimately some form of self-hatred. So we spend the rest of our lives trying to escape this pain through one of the devices described above. Or we try to assume an appearance that will please others and gain us loving acceptance. We give up on being ourselves and play at being someone else, someone who will be worthy of recognition and love.

What Does It Mean to Love Yourself?

When I was young and very zealous, I once told an older and wiser man that I was going to spend all my life and all my energies loving others. He gently asked if I was going to love myself with equal determination. I protested that loving others would leave no time for loving myself. It sounded very saintly. However, my older and wiser friend looked at me long

and pensively. Finally he said, "You are on a suicide course."
My facile reply was: "What a nice way to go, eh?" But, of
course, he was right. I now know what he knew all the time:
true love of others is premised on a true love of oneself.

To understand what it means to love oneself, let us first ask
what it means to love another. In the following chapter I
would like to investigate the deeper meanings and implications of love. For now let us say only that love does at least
these three things:

1 Love esteems and affirms the unconditional and unique
   value of the one loved.
2 Love acknowledges and tries to fulfill the needs of the
   one loved.
3 Love forgives and then forgets the failings of the one
   loved.

When we are asked to "love our neighbor as ourselves," the
clear implication is that whatever we would do for our
neighbor we would *also* and *first* do for ourselves. In other
words, it's a package deal. You have two people you must love:
yourself and your neighbor. You can't really love one without
loving the other.

To understand how this would work in actual practice, it
might help to think of those persons whom you truly love.
Stand off at a distance from them, and ask yourself: Have I
really tried to see and affirm my unconditional and unique
value as I see and affirm theirs? Do I really try to consider and
fulfill my own needs the way I fulfill theirs? Have I really
forgiven myself for my faults and mistakes as I have forgiven
theirs? Think about it. Do you think of yourself as gently and
lovingly as you do those others in your life whom you love
most? Do you offer yourself the same kind of warmth and
understanding that you offer them?

One final example. Let us say that someone else asks you a favor. Now, love asks you to try to fulfill your friend's need, but there is also someone else that you must consider with equal attention: yourself. Let us look at your needs. One of your primary needs is to go out in love to others. The only way to be loved is to be loving. The only truly happy people are those who have found someone, some cause to love and belong to. However, you may have other needs to be considered. You may need rest, or you may have another pressing duty, and so on. It may be that, all things considered, you will have to refuse your friend's request.

What I am describing is not self-preoccupation or narcissism. It is simply a description of a balanced love, extended with the same concern to self and to neighbor. The balance can shift, so that we give all our concern only to self or attempt to give all our concern only to our neighbor. But neither of these attitudes is humanly viable. Neither is true and balanced love.

The Gospel of Glasser

Whether this basic human need be described as self-love, self-esteem, self-appreciation, or self-celebration (each seems to bring out a different facet), one thing is sure. This need

In other words, it's a package deal.
You have two people you must love:
yourself and your neighbor.

cannot be seriously frustrated without a general breakdown of the whole personality. Dr. William Glasser, author of *Reality Therapy* and one of the bright and innovative psychiatrists of our day, makes two fundamental assumptions about this sense of personal worth. I am sure that he is correct.

The first assumption is that *all* psychological problems, from the slightest neuroses to the deepest psychoses, are symptomatic of the frustration of this fundamental human need for a sense of personal worth. The depth and duration of the symptomatic problems (for example, phobias, guilt complexes, paranoia) are only indicative of the depth and duration of the deprivation of self-esteem.

Glasser's second assumption is that the self-image of any human being will be the radical determining factor of all his or her behavior. True and realistic self-esteem is the basic element in the health of any human personality. People act, and especially relate to other people, in accordance with the way they think of and feel about themselves. Our *interpersonal* problems begin with *intrapersonal* conflicts.

Theoretical assent to these assumptions and to the basic necessity of self-esteem may not be too difficult. However, practical acknowledgment in the dust of daily battle can be a heroic achievement. I can easily trace your obnoxious behavior to the invisible roots of an unsuccessful struggle for self-esteem, until you hurt me. Then my own psychological scars begin to ache, and I stop thinking about you and your needs. I stop trying to understand you and I am tempted to judge you and even to hurt you. I must tell you this. It is very important that you know it. I want to offer you unconditional love. I really know you need it, and I want to fulfill your needs so that you may be fully alive. But I am not always able to do this. I am not able to give you the unconditional love you need. My own needs are too real, too limiting, too crippling.

I can only say that I will do what I can. I can only ask you to be patient with me.

But I want you to know that I do know what you need, even when I cannot always give it to you. My own limitations and weakness will impede my performance. However, I do know that my greatest contribution to your life will be to help you love yourself, to think better and more gently of yourself. I want to help you to accept your own limitations more peacefully in the perspective of your whole person, which is uniquely valuable. Realistically, however, to give you all that you need would require a wholeness in me that I do not have. I cannot always come through for you as you need me to. I am living at the outer rim of my own ideals, hanging on only with great effort. But I can promise you this much. I will try. I will try always to reflect to you your unique and unrepeatable value and worth. I will try to be a mirror to your beauty and goodness. I will try to read your heart, not your lips. I will always try to understand you rather than judge you. I will never demand that you meet my expectations as the price of admission to my heart.

So do not ask me *why* I love you. Such a question could invite only the response of conditional love. I do not love you because you look a certain way or do certain things or practice certain virtues. Only ask me this: "*Do* you love me?" That I can answer: "Yes, oh yes."

The Options

What we are saying here is that human beings will find a satisfying life in proportion to their esteem for and belief in themselves. It would be wonderful if we could simply make a once-and-for-all decision to love and believe in ourselves. Such habitual self-confidence would free us from all the parasites that deprive us of 90 percent of our human potential. But this is clearly impossible. Everybody agrees. We cannot make it alone. I need your love and you need mine. I need to see my worth and beauty in the reflection of your eyes, in the sound of your voice, in the touch of your hand. And you need to see your worth mirrored back to you by me in the same way. We can succeed or fail together, but separate and alone we can only fail.

People without a sense of self-appreciation can only suffer, and when they hurt with this pain, they hurt twenty-four uninterrupted hours a day. We can handle pains that are self-limiting, like headaches or sunburn. We know they will eventually go away. But how can we handle the pain of failure that strikes at the very center of our being and existence? When will this go away?

This most fundamental of all human problems is complicated by the fact that love from others, which is the radical source of self-esteem, cannot be banked as money can. Self-esteem fluctuates. We cannot hang on to yesterday's sources of self-celebration and coast along on them for the rest of life. There must be a fairly constant intake of reassurance from the love of others. When we find ourselves without love and without some external recognition of our own worth, we feel empty, bankrupt. We hurt and we hurt very deep down. We are aware of hurting, but this pain, unlike many other pains, doesn't tell us what we must do. When I touch a very hot object, the pain tells me to pull away quickly. But the pain of self-hatred and worthlessness is too diffuse, harder to understand and interpret. There is no simple "set of directions" built into this pain.

Most people seek relief by distraction, living like barnacles on the TV screen or dissolving themselves in work or play. But distraction is not a permanent solution. It can only be temporary. It only forestalls the eventual foreclosure of pain. So people who have failed to find satisfaction and peace within themselves usually resort to one of four rather permanent options. In outlining these options, Dr. Glasser insists that each represents an attempted escape from the pain of failure as a person. To the extent that we fail to perceive worth in ourselves, we will retreat into one of these analgesic shelters.

Depression. Psychological depression is an emotional state of morbid dejection and sadness, ranging from mild discouragement to utter despair. However, it can be and is used as a surrogate or substitute form of suffering. When a human psychological motor is vibrating with a dangerously violent pain, depression is an idling, a slowing down of the motor. It saves the motor from breaking apart. Depression spares people from the agony of their deeper pain, protects them from the full impact of their unbearable life situation.

It is useless to suggest to people who have sought the refuge of this option that they "cheer up." Subconsciously at least they must reject such a suggestion. If they were to give up their depression and then find no sense of personal worth, they would be thrown back into the scourging pain of personal failure, from which the depression was an attempted escape. The depression was an alternative in desperation, an option, a protection from the shattering, unbearable fact of personal worthlessness.

It was recently reported in midwestern newspapers that a young husband and father, piloting his own plane and taking his family on vacation, lost his way and the plane crashed. The man himself was the only survivor. All the others were killed. The poor man proceeded to arrange the funerals of his loved ones, and when everything was completed, he calmly killed himself. Friends said that he had shown no signs of deep depression. He seemed to be brave and composed in his

moment of grief. The fact of the matter is that if he had been deeply depressed, he probably would not have killed himself. Contrary to what is usually thought, terribly depressed people do not kill themselves. The depression defuses the violence of the emotions that often lead to self-destruction.

Anger and Antisocial Behavior. The second option is anger. When we choose this alternative, we "act out" the bitter sense of failure and frustration that accompany a sense of worthlessness. Anger is almost always the result of a deeper fear and hidden insecurity. When we feel unsuccessful as persons, we can opt to ventilate this pain through antisocial behavior. If the pain is deep enough, we may even kill, but certainly we will be the cause of some kind of trouble. We will find some way to make the lives of others miserable.

Like depression, "acting out in anger" is designed to be a release from the deeper pain of personal failure. The angry, abusive behavior is a veiled expression of frustration, fear, and self-rejection. This kind of "acting out" is often used in psychotherapy. People are encouraged, in some form of psychodrama, to act out their repressed feelings under controlled circumstances and conditions.

Insanity. When failure to find love and a sense of worth in the real world becomes too painful, rather than try to

The only truly happy people
are those who have found someone,
some cause to love and belong to.

change ourselves, we may opt to change the world. We can "make up" our own world, inside ourselves, and retreat into that world. Insanity is essentially a loss of contact with reality. The condition of being "split from" reality (schizophrenia) may be regarded as a disease in itself. However, it may well be a subconsciously adopted method of thinking, feeling, and acting which creates a new and personal world, in which one will not have to cope with the problem of personal failure. In this sense insanity is really a choice and much like the retreat into fantasy used by children in their traumatic moments of disappointment. Insanity in many cases is both a choice and an escape, a liberation from a very uncomfortable world and life.

Physical Sickness. Dr. Glasser, with most physicians, believes that the most commonly chosen of all four options is physical sickness. In taking this course people translate the psychological pain of failure into physical symptoms, which are usually much easier to bear. Many sicknesses formerly considered to be organic are coming to be viewed as "psychosomatic" because psychological factors have been found to be so significant in their origin.

Physical illness is easier to bear than the failure to find personal worth because there is less awareness of disgrace and culpability associated with physical sickness. It is easier to say that I have an ulcer than to admit my worthlessness as a person. Also, there is probably involved in this option a throwback to childhood. As children our physical pains and sicknesses usually evoked more sympathy than our personal unhappiness. A scratched knee got more loving attention than hurt feelings or a wounded spirit.

At any rate, it is commonly estimated that 90 to 95 percent of all physical illness is psychological in origin. Even such "objective" illnesses as viral or bacterial infections can be psychologically aided and abetted. Tensions and frustrations lower the immunization and resistance mechanisms of the body, opening the doors to sickness. No doubt, too, auto-suggestion is often involved. It is easier to admit a physical pain than a personal failure.

Dr. Glasser tells an interesting story of a psychotic patient whom he visited on his daily rounds as a psychiatrist in a mental hospital. One day a man who had previously been completely disoriented seemed suddenly to have come back into contact with reality. He looked up at Dr. Glasser and very calmly and deliberately announced that he was sick. Upon examination it turned out that the man actually did have pneumonia. During the period of convalescence from pneumonia all symptoms of insanity disappeared. Only gradually, after recovering completely from the pneumonia, did the symptoms of insanity recur. Glasser's surprising explanation: the man had briefly changed the option by which he was assuaging his personal pain. He had moved from insanity to physical sickness and back again to insanity.

The Addictions

Each of the options described above is an alternative to the admission of failure as a person. However, while each of these options somehow camouflages and alleviates the essential agony, there is still pain. People still hurt, and so, as Glasser points out, they may well turn to some form of painkilling addiction in addition to the original escape option. Alcohol and opium are the most effective painkillers, though they are addictive and destructive. Some people choose a negative or destructive form of addiction, like dope or alcohol. Others choose a neutral addiction like food. Still others choose a form of addiction that is generally considered positive, like work.

So we have, among other victims of addiction, alcoholics, foodaholics, and workaholics. The one thing that they all have in common is that they are trying to dull the pain of an almost worthless existence.

The self-defeating part of all forms of addiction is that if one succeeds and does remove the pain, tranquilized sufferers no longer have the needed impetus to seek and find their own worth as a person. They tend to withdraw from life. One of the most frightening tragedies of our times is the addiction of enormous numbers of people to drugs, many of which have been proclaimed biogenetically destructive. The saddest part of the tragedy is that once people get into drugs, they have crossed a bridge into a world of unreality, and they have burned that bridge behind them. Once they live in unreality, addicts find it difficult to recognize reality, to see things as they really are, to hear them as they really are, and to cope with them as they really are.

Consequently, eminent psychiatrists, such as Viktor Frankl, object to the use of all "high" producing drugs, including marijuana, on the grounds that addicts and even potheads eventually lose the ability to distinguish between reality and illusion, between the facts and their fantasies. Sadly, too, once an addiction has begun to rule its victims, addicts prefer their addiction to everything and everyone else.

Conclusion

Pain in itself is not an evil to be avoided at all costs. Pain is rather a teacher from whom we can learn much. Pain is somehow instructing us, telling us to change, to stop doing one thing or to begin doing another, to stop thinking one way and begin thinking differently. When we refuse to listen to pain and its lessons, all we have left is one of the escapist tendencies of the options and addictions. In effect we have said: I will not listen. I will not learn. I will not change.

When applied to human beings, almost all labels are meaningless. However, I do think that there is one really meaningful distinction, and that is between "growing" and "static-escapist" people. It is a distinction between those who are "open" to growth and those who are "closed." Open and growing people do not begrudge the pedagogy of pain, and are willing to try change. They will initiate appropriate responses and adjustments. Others, for reasons we do not know, simply will not address themselves to the lessons of pain. They rather seek a narcotized and tranquilized existence, a peace without profit. They are willing to settle for 10 percent of their potential. They are willing to die without having really lived.

There is something that a growing person can do, a way to find personal worth, self-esteem, self-appreciation, and a cause to celebrate. We will take this up in the following chapter. Through true and lasting love, we can recover acceptance of self, a realization of our worth. When these are present, everything else will somehow move in the direction of growth on the paths of peace. When love and worth are missing, there is left only a partial existence. We can achieve only a fraction of what might have been. We will die without having really lived. The glory of God—a person fully alive—will forever be diminished.

A thought transfixed me: For the first time in my life I saw the truth as it is set into song by so many poets, proclaimed as the final wisdom by so many thinkers. The truth—that love is the ultimate and highest goal to which man can aspire. Then I grasped the meaning of the greatest secret that human poetry and human thought and belief have to impart: the salvation of man is through love and in love.

Viktor Frankl, *Man's Search for Meaning*

Human needs and the experience of love

Most people are never able to achieve the fullness of life that represents the highest glory of God in humans. They remain forever shackled by doubts, fears, and guilt, trading in pain-dulling options and addictions. The world of advertising plays upon their tortured spirit, promising them treats in taste, blue vacation skies, better mattresses, and so on. They buy these things, hoping to fly now and pay later, until the closets of their lives become cluttered. But the pain goes on throbbing.

Profound change never comes quickly or easily. Modification in habits of behavior, a revision in basic attitudes and life orientation, unknotting old prejudices and running the risk of openness—this is a wide, round curve that can be negotiated only slowly, not a sharp corner that can be turned all at once.

But one thing is clear. All psychological research has established this fact beyond doubt. More important than any psychological theory, teaching, or therapeutic technique, that which heals and promotes human change and growth is a one-to-one relationship of love.

The Anatomy of Effective Love

What is this love that works the miracle of human healing and liberation? Somehow, I think, we know instinctively what love means, both when we are loving and when we are loved. However, it will help to talk more specifically about the nature of love. For a working definition, I would like to use the description of love given by Dr. Harry Stack Sullivan in *Conceptions of Modern Psychiatry*:

> *When the satisfaction, security, and development of another person become as significant to you as your own satisfaction, security, and development, love exists.*

In theory, love implies a basic attitude of concern for the satisfaction, security, and development of the one loved. In practice, love implies that I am ready and willing to forgo my own convenience, to invest my own time, and even to risk my own security to promote your satisfaction, security, and development. If I have the basic attitude of love and I am able to translate it into action, the presumption is that I love you.

*That which heals
and promotes human change and growth
is a one-to-one relationship of love.*

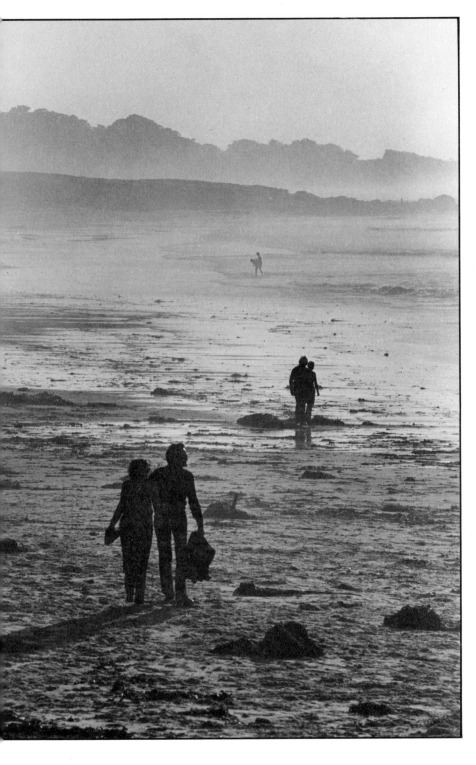

But this is only a working definition of love. There are, in the complicated anatomy of love, many other theses that must be duly acknowledged.

THESIS ONE:
Love Is Not a Feeling

I feel pretty sure that most of the people I know identify love with a feeling or emotion. They "fall in love" and they "fall out of love," in uneven rhythms. The flame of love is extinguished in their lives only until a new match can be struck. I remember a young lady telling me that her husband announced at the end of their honeymoon that he no longer loved her. It was only two weeks after I had witnessed their marriage vows, and so I figured that something was wrong with him or his idea of love either then or now.

Now, everyone knows that feelings are like yo-yos, up and down, depending on such fickle things as the barometer, amounts of sunshine, digestion, the time of the month, and the side of the bed out of which we crawl on a given morning. Feelings are fickle, and people who identify love with feelings become fickle lovers. The French novelist Anatole France once wrote: "In love only the beginnings are delightful. That is why we keep beginning again, falling in love all over again." When we identify love with feelings, we go through life searching for "that old feeling" which crooners have immortalized in song.

It is obvious that feelings *are related to love*. The first attraction of love is usually experienced in terms of very strong feelings. And I cannot—unless I am some kind of hero or masochist—put your satisfaction, security, and development on a par with my own if I do not for the most part have supportive, loving feelings toward you. However, in the course of a love relationship, we will have to go through an occasional winter of emotional discontent to find a newness of our love in the springtime. As the tinsel of young love is burnished by time into the more valuable gold of mature love, there will be times when emotional satisfaction will be absent. There will be other times when negative feelings will cloud the skies of our world; but certainly growth in love supposes and needs generally good emotional weather.

It would be fatal to identify love with a feeling because of the fickleness of feelings. However, it would be equally lethal to a relationship of love if there were no warm and loving feelings to support the intentions of love.

THESIS TWO:
Love Is a Decision and a Commitment

In this chapter, we are considering the interpersonal relationship of love. Such a relationship admits of many levels. I can love and be loved by another as my father or mother, brother or sister, close friend, closest friend and total confidant, husband or wife. The contract of love would be different in each of these cases. Obviously, I cannot have a deep, sharing relationship with many people. There is not enough time, nor do I have the emotional capacity to interact in a deeply personal and loving way with many people. Erich Fromm writes:

> *Love is an activity, not a passive affect; it is a "standing in," not a "falling for." In the most general way, the active character of love can be described by stating that love is primarily giving, not receiving.*

I cannot enter into a love relationship with many people. I would be exhausted in the effort. So I must choose. Of course, there will be certain reciprocal obligations and responsibilities between myself and those to whom I am related by bloodlines, but even here there is room for choice. I can freely and legitimately choose my father or my mother to be my special confidant, one of my brothers or sisters as my special friend. The greatest gift that I have to give to another is my love, and I must carefully choose those in whom I will invest this sacred capacity.

How do I make this decision? All sorts of considerations enter into such decision making, from the amount of things I can share in common with another, our capacity to fulfill each other's needs, temperament, interests, intelligence, values, artistic and athletic abilities, physical appearance, right down to that mysterious thing called "chemistry." All this fits under the heading of "relative compatibility." So I look around at those who are in my world, and make my choices, and offer my love accordingly. There may be somewhere in this universe someone who would be just right for me, tailor-made to all my preferences, but that person may not be in my immediate world, the world from which I must choose those whom I will love.

Since love can exist on many levels, it is extremely important not to offer a commitment of love that I may not be able to honor. Inexperienced and immature people tend to do this, to say things under the impulse of strong emotions or physical reactions (and under the trees at night), which have a hollow sound the next morning after coffee.

The danger of such a premature, undeliberated commitment is this. Most people lurk behind protective walls, what Harry Stack Sullivan calls "security operations." These are designed to protect an already injured ego from further vulnerability. At the call of love, these people come out, perhaps haltingly at first, but they do come out, reassured by the promises of love. If I have made a premature or overstated commitment, I will later have to take back my promises made to such a person. I will have to explain that I really did not mean what I said, or that I have changed my mind. I will leave that person standing painfully naked and unprotected. He or she will return again to the dense forests of a new security operation, go back behind a higher and more impenetrable wall. And, once burned, doubly cautious. It may be a long time before anyone will ever successfully call that person out again, if that be possible at all. People who have experienced only a fragile, conditional, and temporary kind of love will no doubt find the adventure of human life very painful and precarious.

Such care and consideration in making the commitment of love does not, of course, preclude the fact that a young man or woman in search of a marriage partner may well try many relationships before finding the one on which he or she is ready to make a "life wager." Getting to know many people, "dating" many before making the final choice and commitment is obviously a wise procedure. The caution against overstatement of intentions and a premature commitment remains valid, however, especially during this period of experimentation. The old ballad "It's a Sin to Tell a Lie" reminds us of the many broken hearts and broken lives "just because those words [I love you] were spoken."

THESIS THREE:
Effective Love Is Unconditional

Love may be given either conditionally or unconditionally. There is no other possibility. Either I attach conditions to my love or I do not. I would like to say at this point that only unconditional love can effect lasting change in the life of the person to whom that love is offered.

In his work *Conceptions of Modern Psychiatry,* from which we took our working definition of love, Dr. Sullivan talks of the "quiet miracle of developing the capacity of love." He describes being loved as the source of this miracle. The first impulse to change, he says, comes not so much from being challenged as from being loved. Only in an atmosphere of unconditionally offered love will the human barriers to relationships be lowered.

There is a story of a housewife who related that her husband's love seemed to be conditioned on her keeping the house tidy and in order at all times. She maintained that she needed to know that he loved her whether the house was cleaned up or not, in order to have the strength to keep the house clean. If you understand and agree with what she is saying, you understand the point being made here. The only kind of love that helps us change and grow is unconditional.

Immature people say things under the impulse of strong emotions, which have a hollow sound the next morning after coffee.

Conditional love always degenerates into pan-scale love. Both parties are expected, in pan-scale love, to put a donation into the proper pan so that a perfect balance is achieved. But sooner or later some tension, some pain, some struggle will distract one of the pan-scale lovers, and he will not make his monthly payment on time. So the other conditional lover, refusing to be swindled, removes part of her contribution in order to be sure that more isn't going out than coming in—until nothing is left but emotional or legal divorce.

There is another question, and it is not so simple. Can we expect one party in a love relationship to continue making an unconditional contribution and commitment of love without a sustaining response from the other? Theoretically, I believe that if a person could continue offering an unconditional love, the other would in time respond. But perhaps the response would come too late. If the person trying to offer unconditional love is given nothing in response, to nourish the capacity and renew the strength for love, the relationship may be brought to an inevitable failure.

In practice I think this possibility is claimed far more than it actually occurs. People renege on their love commitments, run off to divorce courts, and take to falling in love all over again (with somebody else). They do these things without ever challenging their personal resources, developing their ingenuity, or testing their coping mechanisms. It has been said that love works if we will work at it. I think that this is true, and I think that faithfulness will always be the measure and test of human love.

Footnote: "Unconditional love" should be interpreted as an ideal, a goal toward which true love aspires, but which is realistically not within human reach or attainment. We are all to some extent injured, limited by the throb of our own needs and pains. Only a totally unscarred and free person could consistently give unconditional love. Such a person, of course, does not exist.

THESIS FOUR:
Love Is Forever

This thesis is simply a corollary of the previous thesis. A time limit on love is only one of the conditions we can attach to our commitment. I will love you as long as, until . . . In the movie *Butterflies Are Free,* the superficial, scatterbrained nymphet played so well by Goldie Hawn is portrayed in the act of running away from her blind lover. She explains her flight: ". . . because you are blind. You're crippled!" In the most profound moment of the movie, the young man replies: "No, I am not crippled. I am sightless but not crippled. You are crippled, because you can't commit yourself to anyone. You can't belong."

The commitment of love, at whatever level, has to be a permanent thing, a life wager. If I say that I am your friend, I will always be your friend, not as long as or until anything. I will always be there for you. Effective love is not like the retractable point on a ballpoint pen. If I say I am your man, I will always be your man. In the words of another old song, "When I fall in love, it will be forever."

Any other kind of love loses its effect. I need to know that the love you offer me is a permanent offer before I will give up my security operations, my masks, roles, and games. I cannot come out to a temporary, tentative love, to an offer which has all that fine print and many footnotes in the contract.

THESIS FIVE:

The Commitment of Love Involves Decisions . . .
Decisions . . .
Decisions . . .

We have said that love is a commitment to the satisfaction, security, and development of the one loved. In loving you I am committed to the fulfillment of your needs, whatever they may be. But there is a double difficulty here (I didn't promise you a rose garden!): First of all, your needs are constantly changing. If I love you, I have to be constantly reading your needs, watching you with the look of love. I must be asking: What do you need me to be today, this morning, tonight? Are you discouraged and in need of my strength? Have you experienced some success and are you inviting me to rejoice, to celebrate with you? Or are you lonely and need only my hand softly in yours? This kind of empathetic listening and looking is one of the deepest challenges of effective love. It is not easy to know who you are at any given moment and what you may need me to be.

The second difficulty involved in the practice of love is this. It is I, not you, who must decide what you need me to be. I cannot simply ask you and trust you to know. It may well be

*Conditional love always degenerates
into pan-scale love.*

that, according to my lights, the most loving thing for me to do is to tell you a truth that you do not want to hear. Love may ask me to stay by your side even when you are angrily telling me to go away, or to resurrect an unsettled discussion that you want to abandon in disgust. In taking on the responsibility for these decisions, I will be right sometimes and I will be wrong sometimes. More important, however, than the rightness or wrongness of my judgments will always be the fact that I did what I did because I loved you. I wanted what was best for you. I chose to feel somehow responsible for your life and growth and the development of all your human powers.

Of course, my decisions must never in any way preempt your freedom. I must be me and offer my gift. At the same time I must let you be you, free to accept or to reject my gift. This is perhaps the most difficult line that true love must walk, being myself and offering my contributions according to my lights and yet never forcing your acceptance or response.

THESIS SIX:
The Essential Gift of Love Is a Sense of Personal Worth

If what we have said in chapter one is true—that the ability to feel good about one's self, to love, appreciate, and celebrate one's own goodness is the key factor in the health of human personality and the basic ingredient of human happiness—then the essential contribution of love is clear. My love must empower you to love yourself. We should judge our success in loving not by those who admire us for our accomplishments, but by the number of those who attribute their wholeness to our loving them, by the number of those who have seen their beauty in our eyes, heard their goodness acknowledged in the warmth of our voices. We are like mirrors to one another. We cannot know what we look like until we see our reflection in some kind of mirror. It is an absolute human certainty that we cannot know our own beauty or perceive a sense of our own worth until it has been reflected back to us in the mirror of another loving, caring human being.

THESIS SEVEN:

Love Means the Affirmation, Not the Possession, of the One Loved

A sense of a person's own worth is no doubt the greatest gift we can offer to another. It is the greatest contribution we can make to any life. We can give this gift and make this contribution only through love. However, it is essential that our love be liberating, not possessive. We must at all times give those we love the freedom to be themselves. Love affirms others *as other*. It does not possess and manipulate them *as mine*. Pertinent here is the quotation of Frederick Perls: "You did not come into this world to live up to my expectations. And I did not come into the world to live up to yours. If we meet it will be beautiful. If we don't, it can't be helped."

In Old English the word for love is *frēon,* from which the word *friend* is derived. To love is to liberate. Even in the structure of the language there is an implication that love and friendship are freeing. Love and friendship must empower those we love to become their best selves, according to their own lights and visions.

This means that wanting what is best for you and trying to be what you need me to be can be done only in a way that preserves your freedom to have your own feelings, think your own thoughts, and make your own decisions. If your personhood is as dear to me as my own, which is the implication of love, I must respect it carefully and sensitively. When I affirm you, my affirmation is based on your unconditional value as a unique, unrepeatable, and even sacred mystery of humanity.

In evaluating my love for you, I must then address myself to the question of whether my love is in fact possessive and manipulative or really affirming and freeing. It will help, in this evaluation, to ask myself these questions: Is it more important to me that you be pleased with yourself or that I be pleased with you? Is it more important that you attain the goals you have set for yourself, or that you attain the goals I want for you?

Another test is this: To the extent that I truly love and affirm you, you will be enabled to relate more successfully to other people, and I will rejoice in this. I will want you to love others and others to love you. I will not want to become "your whole life." A person "fully alive" will relate well to many people and enjoy a great variety of things. My love must affirm and free you to live fully, to be alive in all your parts and powers, to experience fully the range of heavenly glory that fills our world.

The Dynamics of Love

So far we have said that the essential factor in human personality adjustment and the wellspring of the fullness of life is true appreciation and celebration of oneself. Where this is present, peace and joy will abound. Where this is absent, there will be sad attempts to escape into options and addictions in an effort to dull the edge of pain. Consequently, if we truly love others and want their satisfaction, security, and development, this sense of personal worth will be the chief contribution we can make to the persons loved and to the fullness of their lives. After having defined the nature and function of love, we would like to investigate now the dynamics of love, the process and experience which alone can result in a secure self-image. Only love can confer an abiding sense of personal worth and the consequent joy that will fill the whole of a human life.

The very nature of humans is dialogical. Human life is a basic relatedness. The I of one is in constant search of the Thou of another and the We of a love relationship. The success or failure of this search is the essential success or failure of a human life. To be human is to love and to be loved. The basic cause of all mental and emotional illness is the inability to form deep and lasting human relationships of love.

The innate need to be loved is revealed in the earliest moments of infancy. The feeling of being wanted and the satisfaction of belonging are absolute requirements from the very moment a person is born into this world. There is a universal agreement that the amount of affection received in infancy determines, more than any other influence, the whole course and quality of a human life. Dr. Lee Salk is a pediatric psychologist. In his book *What Every Child Would Like His Parents to Know,* he summarizes and presents the evidence and argument that our physical and psychological welfare is very largely a product of affectionate, demonstrative love received in infancy.

Later, during childhood, many youngsters are bothered by the fantasy that they are not wanted and will even play games to get reassurance. Temper tantrums, threats to run away from home, antisocial behavior—all are thinly veiled appeals for that basic knowledge so essential to human life: a sense of personal worth as recognized only in being loved. Parents should, in every way possible, assure children of their worth and their lovability. Only when children know that they are *loved* can they get to that necessary truth about themselves, that they are *lovable*. And only when they really believe that they are lovable will they then anticipate and expect friendliness and love from others during the course of life. It is in this secure condition and expectation that children are enabled to go out lovingly and trustingly to others, to run the risks of loving and being loved.

If children are not sufficiently assured, they will of course doubt their own lovability and consequently be doubtful about the reception they will get from others. It is inevitable that such insecurity will lead to defensive, self-protective games, to what Dr. Sullivan calls "security operations." The call to human relatedness, to encounters of love, so deeply implanted in our dialogical nature, will be frustrated in such a life. And the very buffers set up to protect the aching ego from further damage will also prevent the actual human contact and interaction of love.

After a hopefully liberating assurance from their family during childhood, children will in the early school years seek companions of the same sex with whom they will test their newfound capacity for making friends. But the most important kind of love—love that promotes human maturity and wholeness—will open to them at the onset of adolescence: friendship with a person of the opposite sex. The word *sex* is from the Latin verb *secare,* which means "to cut." The implication is that God, having made human nature, cut it in half, into male and female. The whole personalist theory of heterosexuality implies that neither half can be whole without somehow being joined to the other half. e.e. cummings writes: "one's not half two. it's two are halves of one." Any individual, in order to actualize his or her potential as a human being, must have the experience of true and deep friendship with a person of the opposite sex. While this does not imply genital sexual experience, there is really no such thing as a "purely platonic" relationship in any real friendship between a man and a woman, from adolescence onward. In every such relationship sex will always be a strong element and force, either consciously or subconsciously.

Observing the proper precautions where and when needed, we should accept this sexual drive as a healthy and wholesome force that leads to a deeper actualization of the whole human personality and the capacity for life. The sex drive—and again I am referring to general not genital sexuality—offers a new vitality, a new quality to relatedness. This is something we have all experienced in the presence of a person of the opposite sex. A new part of us seems to come alive, and it is a fact that something has been awakened and enlivened in us.

Depth psychologists, following Carl Jung, tell us that there is a male *(animus)* and a female *(anima)* component or function in every human personality. To be a fully alive or "individuated" (Jung's term) human being, both components must be brought into conscious harmony. In the normal man, due to the learned behavior of our present culture, the male component is conscious but the female unconscious. The reverse is true for a woman.

The male component or sexual function of the soul engages predominately in things of the head and will: order, logic, power, courage, protection, dependability. The female component is associated with the things of the heart: art, music, religion, nature, flowers. Its main endowments are what we think of as "feminine" qualities.

It is obvious that the more both components are awakened and developed in any given individual, the more fully alive that person will be and the more fully he or she will experience all that is good, real, and beautiful in the world. Depth psychologists assure us that this awakening of the female component in a man and the male component in a woman, so essential to human wholeness, can take place only in a relationship of love with a person of the opposite sex.

A person of the opposite sex more easily calls me out of the protection of my security operations and my endless pre-occupation with self, and introduces me to the possibilities of a relationship of real caring. I feel more secure with a person of the opposite sex in one respect at least, that the other is not so obviously my competitor or an object of comparison. It is consequently easier for me to confide in a person of the opposite sex, to admit my hiddenness, to risk transparency. At least, this is the usual human experience.

The Counterfeits of Love

Love between a man and a woman can and should be the most liberating, maturing, and fulfilling experience of adult human life. However, the kind of profound union from which such blessings come is not an easy achievement. The Spanish existentialist philosopher Ortega y Gasset describes three different counterfeit versions of this love that can exist between a man and a woman. The counterfeit versions distort rather than develop human personality.

The Physical Conquest. In the first counterfeit of love, one or both of the partners see the other primarily as a source of physical, sexual pleasure. The details and concessions of the whole relationship are all arranged to maximize the possibilities and opportunities for physical gratification. The partner is "used," perhaps even willingly and without deception, as a source of bodily pleasure. Whatever protests to the contrary are raised, the partner is viewed only as a thing, an object, a condition and source of self-gratification.

The Psychological Conquest. This second delusory fiction of love is less obvious but more perverse than the first counterfeit of love. The goal here is psychological conquest. The bright lines and the right moves are here more subtle, designed to seduce the partner psychologically, to get him or her to fall in love, to fall at the feet of the conqueror, to be dominated and submissive not just as a body but as a person. When this strategy succeeds, the supposed "lover" almost immediately loses interest in the other who has been won over. He or she becomes just one more mounted trophy in the game room of the mind. "When the fish is in the boat, the fun is all over."

The Projected Image. Usually, when a man and a woman first "fall in love," it is not with the reality of the other person but with a "projection" of what a loved one should be. It may be that the projected image is derived from a mother or father or a dream. Carl Jung says that "every man carries his Eve in himself," meaning that every man carries in his subconscious the image of what a lovable woman is. Likewise, of course, every Eve carries her Adam within herself. This explains why certain men "fall for" certain types of women, and vice versa. The image projected may, in some cases, have very little relationship to the real person. The problem with this is that if the person insists on keeping the image and making the other conform to it, he or she will love only an image, only a projection, and will not even get to know the other person.

Genuine Love

Two solitudes that protect, touch, and greet each other. Here we find the only reality worthy of the name love. The two partners drop, however gradually, the projected image, which was the first source of attraction, to find the even more beautiful reality of the person. They are willing to acknowledge and respect *otherness* in each other. Each person values and tries to promote the inner vision and mysterious destiny of the other. Each counts it a privilege to assist in the growth and realization of the other's vision and destiny. Rilke's brilliant poetic insight seems to capture the nature of the true love relationship:

> Love is . . . a high inducement to the individual to
> ripen, to become something in himself, to become a
> world, to become world to himself for another's sake.
> It is a great, an exorbitant demand upon him,
> something that chooses him out and calls him to vast
> things. Love consists in this, that two solitudes protect
> and touch and greet each other.

Conclusion

When the encounter and relationship of true love are missing in human life, it is usually because people have either selfishly or timidly kept the doors of their hearts locked and barricaded. They are either unable or unwilling to risk transparency, to expose the most sensitive areas of their souls

Answering the call to love
demands much courage and determination
because self-exposure always involves a risk
of being seriously hurt.

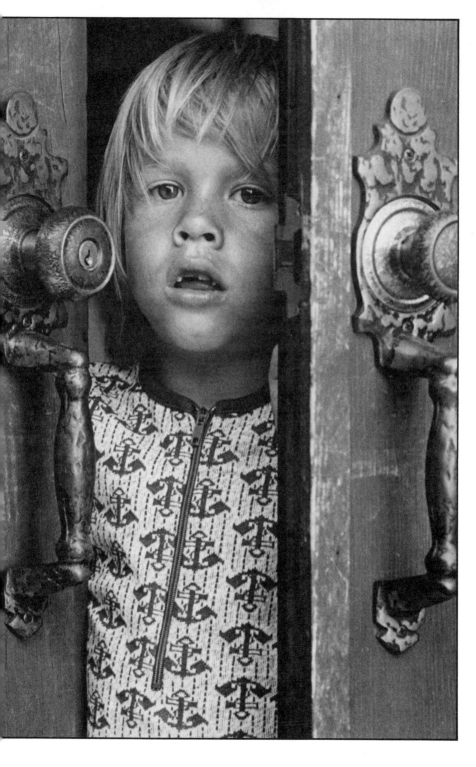

to another. Without such willingness to risk, human life can be only a prolonged pain of starvation and the whole world only a bleak prison. Answering the call to love demands much courage and determination because self-exposure always involves a risk of being seriously hurt. But without transparency, love is impossible, and without love, human life is seriously incomplete.

When people take the risk of loving, their love will usually be returned. Those who are willing to love will eventually find love. And then the mirror will be there, the mirror reflecting back the image of a loving person, and this is the beginning of true self-esteem and self-celebration. This is why Viktor Frankl says that the origin of true self-esteem is in "the reflected appraisal of those whom we have loved."

It has been well said that the *second hardest* thing in all the world is to engage in the challenging process of living intimately and growing with another. The *hardest* thing in all the world is to live alone. If love is anything, it is a gradual process, the long round curve that must be carefully negotiated, not the sharp right-angle turn that is made in an instant, once and for all. A man or a woman must set out upon a long journey and walk many miles to find the joys of love. They will have to pass through deep and dark forests and there will be many dangers. They will have to be careful of love as they are of few other things. Love will demand abstinence from all that might prove poisonous to love. Love will demand much courage, perseverance, and self-discipline.

But the journey to love is the journey to the fullness of life, for it is only in the experience of love that we can know ourselves. Only by loving can we joyfully accept what we are and will become, and find the fullness of life that is the glory of God. Only in love can we find cause for perennial celebration.

It was the day my father died. It was a bleak, cold, and blustery day in January. In the small hospital room, I was supporting him in my arms, when his eyes suddenly widened with a look of awe I had never seen before. I was certain that the angel of death had entered the room. Then my father slumped back, and I lowered his head gently onto the pillow. I closed his eyes, and told my mother who was seated by the bedside, praying:

"It's all over, Mom. Dad is dead."

She startled me. I will never know why these were her first words to me after his death. My mother said:

"Oh, he was so proud of you. He loved you so much."

Somehow I knew from my own reaction that these words were saying something very important to me. They were like a sudden shaft of light, like a startling thought I had never before absorbed. Yet there was a definite edge of pain, as though I were going to know my father better in death than I had ever known him in life.

Later, while a doctor was verifying death, I was leaning against the wall in the far corner of the room, crying softly. A nurse came over to me and put a comforting arm around me. I couldn't talk through my tears. I wanted to tell her:

"I'm not crying because my father is dead. I'm crying because my father never told me that he was proud of me. He never told me that he loved me. Of course, I was expected to know these things. I was expected to know the great part I played in his life and the great part I occupied of his heart, but he never told me."

C H A P T E R   T H R E E

Love and communication

No matter how romanticists have tried to color it ever sweet, and despite the sardonic claim of cynics that it is overrated, love is the tough, essential answer to the riddle of human existence. It is the essential component of human wholeness and happiness. To live is to love. Still it must be conceded that the cynics have a good set of statistics. It's not just the backlog of business in the divorce courts. It's the general fragmentation of the human family, parents against children, brothers against brothers, and so on. If love really is the answer, it seems quite certain that the efforts of humans to find this answer in love relationships have a high mortality rate. Love works if people will work at it. But why does love so often fail? What is the "work" that love demands, and why are we sometimes unwilling to undertake it?

The "Work" of Love

Love supposes, is, and does many things, but basically it is practiced in the act of *sharing*. To the extent and depth that

---

C H A P T E R   T H R E E

Love and communication

No matter how romanticists have tried to color it ever sweet, and despite the sardonic claim of cynics that it is overrated, love is the tough, essential answer to the riddle of human existence. It is the essential component of human wholeness and happiness. To live is to love. Still it must be conceded that the cynics have a good set of statistics. It's not just the backlog of business in the divorce courts. It's the general fragmentation of the human family, parents against children, brothers against brothers, and so on. If love really is the answer, it seems quite certain that the efforts of humans to find this answer in love relationships have a high mortality rate. Love works if people will work at it. But why does love so often fail? What is the "work" that love demands, and why are we sometimes unwilling to undertake it?

The "Work" of Love

Love supposes, is, and does many things, but basically it is practiced in the act of *sharing*. To the extent and depth that two people are committed to each other in a love relationship, to that extent and on that level they must actively share each other's life. Another word for sharing is *communication,* the act by which people share something or have it in common. If I communicate a secret of mine to you, we then share it, have it in common. To the extent that I communicate myself as a person to you and you communicate yourself to me, we share in common the mysteries of ourselves. Conversely, to the extent that we withdraw from each other and refuse mutual transparency, love is diminished.

In this context, communication not only is the lifeblood of love and the guarantee of its growth, but is the very essence of love in practice. Love is sharing and sharing is communication. So when we say that communication is the "secret of staying in love," what we are really saying is that the secret of staying in love is to love, to keep sharing, to keep living out one's commitment. Of course, there is a first "yes," a first commitment made to love, but this first "yes" has an endless number of smaller "yeses" inside it.

One of the most common escapes from the practice of realities like love is the substitution of discussion for doing. We would rather debate, think about, and question these realities than put them into practice. It is much easier to discuss truths than to live them. Today, for example, there is much discussion about Christianity as a way of life: Can we still believe? What do we really believe? Is faith essential to happiness? The most obvious failing in the whole history of Christianity is that we have wandered into abstract and endless discussions instead of putting faith into practice. Uncommitted onlookers have been begging us not to entertain them with a debate about our doubts. They are saying: Show me what it would be like if I did believe and commit myself.

It is the same way with love. We would rather discuss it than live it. There is no price of admission to the forums of discussion, but the practice of love is a costly discipleship. Dag Hammarskjold writes in his book *Markings:*

> The "great" commitment all too easily obscures the "little" one. But without the humility and warmth which you have to develop in your relations to the few with whom you are personally involved, you will never be able to do anything for the many. Without them, you will live in a world of abstractions, where . . . your greed for power, and your death-wish lack the one opponent which is stronger than they—love. . . . It is better for the health of the soul to make one man good than "to sacrifice oneself for mankind."

Unity Not Happiness

In rendering to love its required "work" or effort, it is important that we seek unity, not happiness. Those who set out upon the journey of love must strive for that transparency, that sharing and community of life which is the heart of love. Would-be lovers must not be constantly taking their tempera-tures and counting their heartbeats to keep an up-to-the-minute check on how well they feel or how happy they are. A sense of well-being and happiness, as Viktor Frankl so often warns us, can come into a human life only as a by-product. You have no doubt heard this verse:

> Happiness is like a butterfly.
> The more you chase it, the more it will elude you.
> But if you turn your attention to other things,
> It comes and softly sits on your shoulder.

To be truly happy in love, a person must want unity, one-ness, sharing. Sometimes this unity involves many things that are painful: honesty when you would rather lie a little, talking out when you would rather pout, admitting embarrassing feelings when you would rather blame someone else, standing there when you would rather run, admitting doubt when you would rather pretend certainty, and confronting when you would rather settle for peace at any price. None of these things, which are among the just demands of love, brings immediate peace and happiness; they first bring pain and struggle. Yes, love works if we will work at it. The work of love is to achieve a total honesty and transparency, and these are very difficult attainments. So people who chase after the butterfly of happiness in love relationships will be empty-handed and empty-hearted in the end. Unity, not happiness, is the stern condition of success at love.

Dialogue vs. Discussion

I would like to introduce here a distinction, based on content, between two types of communication. The first is the communication or sharing of emotions or feelings, which I would like to call *dialogue*. The second type of communication is the sharing of thoughts, values, the making of plans or decisions together, and, in general, things of a predominantly intellectual nature. This I would like to call *discussion*. Of course, this is an arbitrary distinction, and I am sure that not everyone would accept my usage of the words. It really is not important if others like or want to use the distinction, as long as what I am trying to say is clear. I need this or some such distinction to make a point that I think is tremendously important.

My point is this: There must be an emotional clearance (dialogue) between two involved partners in a love relationship before they can safely enter into a deliberation (discussion) about plans, choices, values. The assumption behind this distinction and the priority given to dialogue is that the breakdown in human love and communication is *always* due to *emotional* problems. Two people in love can continue to deepen in their affection for each other while holding opposite opinions in almost any area of life. These contrary intellectual persuasions do not become an obstacle to love until one or both of the parties feel emotionally threatened.

In the first chapter of this book, we said that the essential need of human nature is self-esteem, self-appreciation, and self-celebration. I can give up almost anything while holding myself and my world together, but I cannot forfeit self-esteem without profound repercussions in my whole life. Most of us have a whole gamut of emotions, especially emotions and expressions of hostility, ready to be detonated in case of threat to self-esteem. Anger in a love relationship almost always arises because we have somehow felt threatened and afraid. My feeling of worth, the joy of being me, and the inner cause I have for self-celebration have been endangered. It is as simple as that; it is as complicated as that. But the point here is that while my emotions are throbbing with these fears, angers, and self-defensive urges, I am in no condition to have an open-minded, honest, and loving discussion with you or with anyone else. I will need the emotional clearance and ventilation of dialogue before I will be ready for this discussion.

The detour that must at all costs be avoided is to mistake an issue that belongs to discussion—for example, how much you spent for that new coat or whether I fixed the broken door—for the real gut issue of personal security, which belongs in the realm of dialogue. Lovers, it has been said, rarely argue about the *real* issue.

We have said that love, unlike money, cannot be banked. There must be a continuous, mutual, and reciprocal support of personal worth in a love relationship. When there is prolonged deprivation of this reinforcement, the "bankrupt" feeling sets in. Then the accompanying options to ease the pain of the feeling of this fundamental failure seem attractive. The problem is, of course, essentially *emotional:* how do I *feel* about myself, my worth, my life? Everything else is symptomatic. All other emotional turbulence, whatever form it takes, is only an outward ripple from this central agony.

More often than not, we fail to realize that our problems are basically emotional, and that we suffer most from those emotions that arise when our sense of worth is threatened. The consequence of this lack of awareness is the so-called "displaced emotion." The way I am treated at my place of work or at my school may cause me to doubt my own worth, with the resultant fear that no one could really esteem, love, or care about me. This is the kind of threat to selfhood that usually surfaces not as fear (which it really is) but as hostility, a self-defensive anger. When enough of this anger gathers in us, without the release and perspective afforded by dialogue, the setting is ripe for displacement of emotions. The kid leaves a roller skate in the driveway, the wife is late with dinner, or the sympathetic question of a well-intentioned parent is interpreted as "being nosey"—and all hell breaks loose. We are, of course, perfectly sure that our hostility is righteous indignation, the kind Jesus felt when he threw the buyers and sellers out the Temple. Anyone would get angry, we are sure, under such circumstances. But the anger and frustration we feel is really displaced. At its roots, the problem is the same old one. We feel somehow diminished in self-respect and we are acting out our anger on the nearest available victim.

Dialogue:
The Gift of Self

We have been saying that dialogue must precede discussion because the static of unresolved and unexpressed emotions will block all attempt at the open, free-flowing exchange that leads to plans, decisions, and so forth. The presumption has been that these emotions are negative, and obviously not all emotions are negative. In the case of positive emotions, there is an even more compelling motive to practice dialogue before discussion. I become a transparent, knowable individual to you only when I tell you my feelings. My ideas, convictions, values, persuasions are really not original with me. I have got them from reading, by inhaling traditions, by listening to and imitating others, by the inevitable osmosis of human contagion. My ideas and the stances I take can locate me in a category, like "Irish," "Catholic," or "Democrat," but they can never make me transparent and knowable, so that you can experience the real me, share my person. Only my feelings, positive-negative-neutral, do this. My feelings are like my fingerprints, the color of my eyes, and the sound of my voice: unique to me and unrepeatable in anyone else. To know me you must know my feelings. And only after you know *me* through dialogue, at any moment in my life, will you be able to understand my ideas, preferences, and intentions, shared in discussion.

If you think for a moment about this, you will realize the truth involved. Perhaps you know someone, a teacher, a neighbor, a local pastor, anyone who trades in ideas, theories, teachings, techniques. If this person keeps his or her communications carefully sterilized and bloodless, strained completely of all emotional content, such a person somehow remains anonymous. I once listened to such a man for eight days, in a series of lectures, and I was sure at the end that I did not know him at all. I wasn't even sure whether he was parroting a book he had read, and I wondered how old his "notes" were and to how many people he had read them. I have noticed that when I myself am the public speaker, audiences "turn on" when I am willing to offer them my feelings, not as a demagogue seeking to manipulate, but quietly as a brother wanting to share. I have watched this truth proved again and again in public forums, in classrooms, in living room conversation, and in one-to-one communication. My emotions are the key to me. When I give you this key, you can come into me, and share with me the most precious gift I have to offer you: myself.

Important Footnote: The emphasis in this section on dialogue is on the communication of emotions. The central thesis is that when I tell you my emotions or feelings, I am telling you who I really am. I am giving you myself. While all this is absolutely true, it might at the same time seem to be saying that you *are* your emotions. This is not true at all. You and I are much more than our emotions. We have fears, but we are more than fear. We get angry, but we are more than our angers. We have minds to know, to make decisions, to accept and absorb values. We have wills, too, the heart to love and belong, to be committed and loyal. Please read, if you have time, what I have written in *Why Am I Afraid to Tell You Who I Am?* on the integration of the emotions by the mind and will. As essential as our emotions are to communication, they do *not* make our decisions for us. Only the perpetual child is ruled by his or her feelings.

Still it is true and cannot be emphasized too much that only when I share my feelings in gut-level communication am I truly sharing myself. It is true that my values, beliefs, and goals are more important than my feelings, but only when I tell you how I feel about my values, beliefs, and goals will you be able to perceive my uniqueness. It is true that my love is more important than my feelings, but only when I share with you the many feelings that my love stirs in me will you be able to see my love as unique and unrepeatable. The diamond is the person, but the setting that brings out and illustrates all the facets of beauty is the feelings. Without the setting the diamond couldn't be seen and admired. Without the feelings, the person cannot be known.

The "Peak" Experience

At each point in our lives we represent a confluence of many things. At the center, of course, is the self-image, but feeding into this central fact of personhood, like spokes moving toward a hub, are many other currents and forces. These are the people and events in our lives, which can be sources of great personal enrichment. However, in the defensive posture of those who have had their egos dented and do not want to risk further vulnerability, most of us move into one security operation or another. We guardedly filter the reality that gets through to us from these currents and forces in our lives. And so life goes on for most of us, pretty much on a plateau. Each yesterday begins to look a lot like today, and each today will resemble tomorrow. Life becomes a series of carbon copies. This is the setting for stagnation in which there is nothing left but to look for a few "kicks," or collect status symbols to be looked at as an old football hero looks at his trophies. This is the portrait of people who are only 10 percent alive, who were made to travel on eight cylinders but who are using only one.

It would be futile to confront such people. Confrontation would very probably only scare them, and they would have

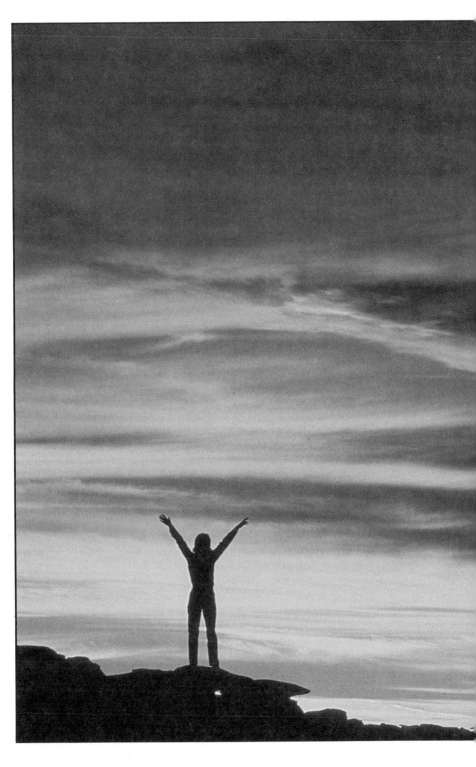

to react angrily, to launch out in some kind of a hostile offense, which is said to be the best defense. They would ask us: "Who the hell do you think you are, anyway?" Sensitivity sessions, so popular in the sixties, that have tried this brutal, frontal assault on human security operations have been reviewed as more dangerous than helpful. So-called "teachable" moments are rarely if ever occasioned by ripping off masks, leaving people nakedly aware of their own failures. There is an enormous risk that they would only go deeper inside themselves.

We get out of the rut, above the plateau, out of a living death, only through "peak" experiences of communication. In a fuller perspective, occurrence or nonoccurrence of these peak experiences is what makes or breaks a love relationship. Without these moments of breakthrough into new and mutual transparency, love becomes dull, stagnant, and boring. Lovers start scratching around elsewhere, looking for some action, some ego stimulation. In the garden of humanity what is not growing is dying.

Let me try now to describe what I mean by peak experience in communication, and then give you an example from my own life. First of all, let us presume that in such a peak experience you open yourself in such a way that your partner

*We get out of the rut
only through "peak" experiences
of communication.*

is called out of himself or herself, and out of all his or her old and fixed positions and calculations, into a new experience. This new experience is not only a deeper knowledge of the reality of you, but also by later refraction and assimilation it will be a new experience for that partner. It will augment the partner's capacity and reality. Such an experience will leave that reality forever changed, and the person more open, more loving, more alive.

Since emotions are what define and reveal the essential me, I will necessarily be revealing my *feelings* in the moment of my transparency. It is the sharing of my feelings that will provide you with the opportunity to know me in a new way, to know yourself in a new way, and to be changed by that knowledge. Perhaps it will be in the context of relating an incident or expressing my love, but it will be the feeling or emotional content that will carry the charge and offer the experience of my person. Unless I open my own unique feelings, you will simply "project" into me your own emotions. For example, if I tell you that I have failed in some way without describing vividly my exact emotional reaction to the failure, you will anticipate that my reaction was what yours would be in a similar situation; and it never, never is. You will, if I deny you my emotional depths, never get to know me, or be enriched by the kind of peak experience being described here.

Why do these peak experiences have such a profound effect? First of all, it is obvious that people are transformed by their relationships with those who are closest to them. Peak experiences of communication inject a new vitality into these relationships. When you open to me a part of yourself—a reaction, a hurt, a tenderness, or a fear that I have never before experienced in you—I am made more aware of your depth and your mystery. I no longer take you for granted, or foolishly believe that I know you so completely that I need not look for anything new, as though you will always be the unchangeable you that I first met and loved.

Second, these peak moments help me to get out of myself. While I am locked inside myself there is no possibility of change. This is just as certain as the old saying that we cannot learn anything new while we are speaking but only when listening. Imprisonment in self is a small, lonely, and incredibly dull world with its population of one. There is no real interaction and so there is no growth or change. When you open the depths of your feelings and yourself to me, it invites me to break away from my preoccupation with myself. It calls me out of the boring sameness that preoccupation with self produces. When this happens, when I go out of myself, the door locks behind me. I can never go back into that small, rigid, fixed little world again. Perhaps such dramatization makes peak experience sound too apocalyptic and the resulting change unrealistically sudden and deep. Change is always slow, but the fact of change and the hope of transformation are very real.

The experience of peak communication may be compared to a man who stays in his apartment alone all day. While there he has a feeling of safety. There is no necessity to interact with other people who may threaten or actually hurt him. He knows where everything is—the night lamp, the bathroom, the Pepto Bismol. He is at least secure from harm in his stagnation. The whole world outside his little apartment is lost on him. He is alive but not very. He is breathing but not really living. Then one day he looks out his window and sees another person who is experiencing a moment of emotional intensity. It is so interesting, so captivating that he forgets about all his fears. He unlocks the door, he goes out to the other, and for that lovely, liberating moment he experiences

another world. He breathes a new and fresh air. The light and warmth of the sun fall on him for the first time. And then he knows something. The life in him has been expanded. He can never go back, never be the same again, or live the same narrow, cramped existence. He wouldn't fit in that world anymore, and all because he has been drawn out of himself to someone else in a profound way. All the dimensions of his world, the anticipations and prejudices in which he has been imprisoned to some extent fall away.

In the wake of peak experiences, both partners are permanently, even if not always dramatically, altered because the whole relationship acquires a new depth and intensity. There will be a new perspective in which each will see the other.

Let me now share with you one such experience from my own life. About five years ago, the doctors told our family that my aged mother very probably had an inoperable cancer of the liver, which had to be considered terminal. To confirm the tentative diagnosis of their tests, the doctors wished to perform exploratory surgery, to which we all agreed. On the night before the surgery, I carefully informed my mother of

Sharing my feelings
will provide you with the opportunity
to know me in a new way,
to know yourself in a new way,
and to be changed.

her condition, so that she could face the mystery of death in a fully human way. I sat nervously on the edge of her hospital bed, and asked if she would like to "go to confession." In the Catholic Church, the members of a priest's family usually go to another priest for the sacrament of Penance, or "confession" as it is popularly called. However, because my mother suffered from a severe arthritis in the latter years of her life, I became her "confessor" of choice for the ten years preceding the time of the episode that I am now relating.

I must also tell you that I was also the youngest of my mother's three children, her "baby." I swear that I could always sense this word in her voice whenever she spoke to me and in her face whenever she looked at me. There was one exception: while she was making one of her angelic "confessions." At this moment I became her "priest," her "Father." At these moments she seemed totally transformed by her faith in me as God's representative. All the sounds and sights of "baby" seemed to disappear.

On the night before the surgery, I heard what I thought might well be her last confession, and as usual it was so saintly that for me it was an exercise in humility. At the conclusion, I assured her that I was bringing to God her sorrow and to her God's forgiveness. To the extent of my ability to be in touch with God and with her, I felt that I must also bring her God's message, the things I thought God would say to her at this face-to-face-with-death moment. The heart of the message I bore was this: "Thank you. Thanks for all the nights you sat up with sick children, for all the silent prayers you said for them, for all the cups of cool water you patiently poured, for all the clothes you sewed and mended, for all the sandwiches you made and wrapped in wax paper, for all the times . . ." She listened attentively and almost dutifully because I was her "Father."

After the absolution and final blessing of the sacramental rite, I instantly became her child again, and she tenderly cupped my bent head in her hands and cradled it in a motherly way on her shoulder. She then turned her lips to my ear: "John," she said, "don't be sad now. Don't be sad for me. If it isn't tomorrow morning, it will be some other morning, and if it isn't this year, it will be some other year. Besides, Daddy's been waiting a long time for me. I am all ready now to go meet him. And you—you have been called to a beautiful life, to do beautiful things for God and for the people you serve. If you feel sad for me, it will take your mind and heart away from your life and your work. Don't let that happen. Don't be sad for me. Remember, if it isn't tomorrow morning, it will be another morning, and if it isn't this year, it will be another. Don't be sad now." Then she kissed me and added: "I gave you up once, and I don't want you back. You belong to God and God's people."

It was like the moment after my father's death. I was crying softly again and couldn't talk, but this time the reason for my tears was different. I had known my mother in this moment more profoundly than ever before, in a moment when she was courageously rising to the occasion of dying, a moment when people are usually reduced to what they really are, no more, no less.

As it turned out, it was not her life that God was asking. The next morning the surgeon came from the operation smiling, assuring us that the suspected cancer was not found, and that the condition causing mother to feel ill was corrected. He said we could see her briefly in the intensive care unit of the hospital. There we found her conscious but cranky. My sister tried to brush back the hairs which had been matted on her forehead, and she complained that the brush was pulling her hair. She even complained that there was no

TV in intensive care. Nothing, not even the good news that she was on the road to recovery, seemed to please her. I stood off at a distance, smiling. "Go ahead, Old Girl," my heart was saying, "let it all out. Your mind is foggy and your body hurts. And that's the way it is in the dust and struggle of daily life. But there is one big difference now. Last night I got to know you. Beneath the words that come out of your mouth without passing through your mind or heart, beneath all the temporary, turbulent, superficial complaints you never really meant, I knew you. And I will always know something about you that will make all of these other moments seem much less important. And some day, when you really have gone to be with God and with Dad, most of all I will remember what you said to me last night, what you meant to me last night."

As the song says, "It only takes a moment to be loved a whole life through." I don't know if this is literally true, but I do believe that the depth and duration of a love relationship will depend on those occasional moments of meeting called "peak experiences."

In Settings of Struggle

The story of my mother is a sweet story with a sweet ending. It could easily mislead one to believe that dialogue is always easy and inevitably leads to peak moments, after which people live happily ever after. It is not so, of course. We must never construe dialogue as a painkilling aspirin or peak experiences as a kind of raw liquor that results in a permanent "high." Laying yourself on the line in the self-disclosure of dialogue will challenge all the courage, determination, and faith that you can muster. The most universal fear of all people is to be found out, to be known and then to be rejected. In fact, I suspect that many people do not hear the vocation to dialogue or refuse to be converted to its gospel of "unity not happiness" because of this fear. We all know that self-revelation is risky. Misunderstanding and rejection really hit where it hurts. But more profoundly, if I admitted to myself the deepest feelings that stir in me, it is possible that I might lose the self-respect and self-appreciation that I need so desperately. It is much easier to *discuss a problem* because I can always change my mind. It is much harder to *expose a feeling* because somehow instinctively I know that I am exposing the place where I really live. It is much easier to give you a box of candy or a box of cigars than to give you myself in self-disclosure. There is very little risk in giving you candy, but when I give you myself, I am putting myself at the mercy of your understanding and acceptance. It is much easier to be busy, very busy, doing a million things for you than to sit down with you trustfully and tell you who I really am, how I really feel about you, about myself, about us, about our past, present and future. But the fact of the matter is that I give you nothing until I give you this gift. There is no other secret of staying in love or growing in love.

One Picture
Worth a Thousand Words

If only I could make a movie of the following true story, it would illustrate better than many words what I am trying to say. A young couple had reached the brink of divorce. The husband, in general a very good and well-intentioned man, had a "weakness," which had bothered him since adolescence but which he had kept carefully concealed from his wife and everyone else . . . till the night he was arrested for his "weakness" and the lid came off.

For several days following the embarrassment of arrest, the young wife and mother reflected on her situation and on the possibility of the future. She decided that she was not equal to this struggle and wanted a divorce. She said that she could not live with the uncertainty of possible future embarrassments. However, she was asked by a counselor to postpone her divorce action on the grounds that her husband's recovery depended more on her loving acceptance of him than on any other human factor or form of therapy. She agreed to try. However, during the next three months there were several recurrences of the problem, although no arrests. In this period her decision became definite: she wanted a divorce.

When they entered the office of the marriage counselor, they were walking at a distance of four or five feet, their eyes carefully avoiding each other. Anger rasped at the edge of their voices.

"I must have a divorce. I can't go on like this!"

"And if she wants a divorce, she can have it. I'm sick and tired of this whole mess, of her hounding. She's always accusing . . ."

It was a clear case of attempted discussion without previous dialogue. The counselor calmly seated the two angry, threatened, and threatening people, and asked for an emotional clearance. He requested that there be no judgments, no accusations, no resurrection of past history. He insisted on straight dialogue: *just feelings.*

The wife began by announcing that her "central" feeling was insecurity. She said she thought that she knew her husband till she found out about this strange weakness which he had hidden from her. She felt that this weakness owned some part of him that was not hers, and this made her jealous. She had personified his weakness and saw it as her competitor. She thought she could have coped with the challenge of another woman, but not this. She was encouraged to continue describing this feeling of insecurity until it became very vivid to all. Both the husband and counselor could feel the texture, taste the loneliness, and hear the agony of her insecurity. Then, by invitation, she continued to describe in a similarly graphic way the other emotions that she was feeling at this time in the context of the problem. She described her sadness, her loneliness, her disappointment in herself and her own lack of strength to cope with the situation. She described an almost constant bewilderment and fear for the future. She felt that the divorce action was an escape. She personally felt like a small child running away from something she just couldn't face.

Judging from his reactions, the husband had heard none of this before. The anger with which he had previously regarded his wife turned into a puzzled, wide-eyed wonder and even hope. After a half hour of excellent description of her feelings, the wife was asked by the counselor if she didn't feel some anger, some desire for vengeance, some desire to hurt her husband in retaliation for the anguish he had caused her. Tears welled up in her eyes, and she admitted that each time the thought of vengeance or retaliation occurred to her, it was immediately drowned in feelings of deep compassion and sorrow, not to mention affection. "I could never deliberately hurt you," she blurted out, "because I love you too much." The eyes of the husband widened. His ears and mind strained to embrace what he was hearing and seeing.

Then, in his time, the husband described his feelings, his central emotion of shame, a feeling of alienation, separation from others. "I have heard and read that others are troubled with my problem, but I am the only one I know of. I feel as though I am different and separated from the rest of the human race. I feel like a leper turned away by society. I feel as if the whole world is having a picnic and I didn't get invited." He graphically described his fear of psychologically infecting his children with his problem, of projecting into them an inclination to the weakness that had made his own life a private hell. He told of putting them out of his lap when this thought and feeling came to terrorize him.

In the most sensitive part of the husband's emotional admission, the wife put a tremulous hand on his knee in a kind of nonverbal way of saying: "I am with you. I will stay with you." Almost as though the floodgates had been opened and there was a feeling of release, the husband went on and on through a whole gamut of emotions: shame, fear, loneliness, alienation, despair. Finally, this man of large muscular stature admitted a strong emotional desire to be held in someone's arms, in the arms of someone with whom he wouldn't be ashamed to cry. He was releasing the little boy who was somewhere inside him.

At this point, both people arose, embraced, and cried together. When the tears were exhausted, they were smiling at each other, looking at each other appreciatively and compassionately. One hour before this they were determined to leave each other forever. After this hour of dialogue, they looked at and held each other as though nothing could ever separate them. They were two good and decent people who almost didn't get to know each other.

This story, too, has a happy ending. But no doubt these people will have many other problems, and perhaps there will even be moments in the future when the bond of their love will again be threatened, but if they have learned the necessity of dialogue as the lifeblood of love, they will be all right. The tinsel will turn into gold.

The partners in a love relationship must realize that a breakdown in communication is emotional in origin. They must learn to share their feelings, to dialogue before attempting discussion. They must be willing to risk transparency in the quest of unity, of knowing and accepting each other. From this alone happiness can result as a by-product. They must be willing to work toward those occasional moments of "peak experience" which vitalize, deepen, and transform a love relationship. With and in such willingness they will learn a valuable secret: the secret of staying and growing in love.

The Marriage Enrichment weekend was over. There was the usual amount of incense in the air, and I enjoyed it. I returned to Chicago with a warm, complacent feeling about all those couples initiated into the art of dialogue, getting to know each other, learning to love each other more deeply. Someone had said to me as I was leaving: "Thanks for giving us to each other." I cherished the compliment all the way back to Chicago, savoring it like an all-day sucker because it expressed my deepest ambition and most sincere intention. Then, after a week, came the following letter:

"You and your damned dialogue! I have just found out that my husband has felt lonely all during the ten years of our marriage. I thought we had a happy marriage. Now I feel like a failure, and he's still lonely. So you open your guts. Then what? You started this. What are you going to do for us now?"

I sat with the letter for a long time, pondering what I would answer.

❧

About those emotions

In learning to understand ourselves we must learn to become open to and accepting of all our emotional reactions. If what we have said about our emotions is the key to personal understanding, then we must learn to listen to our own emotions if we are to become growing persons. There is a basic belief in which I must repose absolute faith in order to understand myself by understanding my emotions. It is this: *No one else can cause or be responsible for my emotions.* Of course, we feel better assigning our emotions to other people. "You made me angry . . . You frightened me . . . You made me jealous . . ." The fact is that you can't make me anything. You can only *stimulate* the emotions that are already in me, waiting to be activated. The distinction between *causing* and *stimulating* emotions is not just a play on words. The acceptance of the truth involved is critical. If I think you can make me angry, then when I become angry I simply lay the blame and pin the problem on you. I can then walk away from our encounter learning nothing. I conclude only that you were at fault because you made me angry. Then I need to ask no questions of myself because I have laid all the responsibility at your feet.

If I accept the thesis that others can only *stimulate* emotions already latently present in me, any experience that produces these emotions becomes a learning experience. I then ask myself: Why was I so afraid? Why did that remark threaten me? Why was I so angry? Was my anger really a disguised way of saving face? Something was already in me that this incident called forth. What was it? People who really accept total responsibility will begin dealing with their emotions in a profitable way. They will no longer allow themselves the easy escape into the judgment and condemnation of others. They will grow as they get more and more in touch with themselves.

In Every Emotion
a Self-revelation

I remember receiving a very bitter letter several years ago. The author of the letter accused me of being a "sadist . . . a bully . . . a megalomaniac . . ." My reaction was actually mild and sympathetic. I knew the writer of the letter must have deep problems, and I wondered how I could help him. The letter stirred in me only compassion. I felt no negative emotions because I did not believe the accusations. I know that I am not a sadist or a bully. I am not even a megalomaniac. The incident helped me to discover in myself a deep and warm compassion.

Several weeks later I was happily bantering with two of my students, and in the playful interchange one of them remarked, "Do you know that you come across to some people as a phony?" Suddenly playtime was over. I pompously demanded a definition of "phony." The two embarrassed students tried to back away, insisting that they themselves didn't think of me as a phony. But this was not enough. A gush of white-hot anger had arisen in me, and I pressed on for a definition. Finally one of the students said, "I guess being a phony means that you don't practice what you preach."

Have anticipated such a definition, I immediately pleaded guilty. I knew that I was on safe ground, being able to point out that no one really lives up to ideals or translates intentions perfectly into action. Then I pointed out a second meaning of *phony,* namely, that people do not practice what they preach because they do not even believe what they preach. To this charge I solemnly pleaded innocent. The bloodletting completed with surgical precision, I dismissed my victims. Of course, I realized immediately that I had been very angry and that I had been unfair because of my anger.

This is the critical moment. The only real mistake is the one from which we learn nothing. In the aftermath of an encounter such as I have just described, there are two options. One can go off in a huff, ranting and raving about others, or one can look inward to find the reason for the emotions that were triggered. This is the essential difference between a growing and a nongrowing person, between authenticity and self-deception. On this one occasion, at least, I chose to be growing and authentic. I looked within myself, and listened carefully to the anger which was gradually subsiding, and I found that it grew out of a deep-seated fear in me that maybe I am a phony, even in the second sense. I could react mildly in the face of an accusation that I am a sadist, a bully, or a megalomaniac, but the accusation of being a phony touches an exposed nerve ending in me. Sometimes I am afraid that I talk a much better game than I am able to live, with the subsequent fear that maybe I don't fully believe all that I preach. I even located some examples to substantiate this. (P.S. I did apologize to the students. I admitted to them the source of my anger and explained what I had found out about myself.)

We are saying that there is something already in us that explains our emotional reactions, but this does not mean that what is in us is bad or regrettable. The fear I have that there is a discrepancy between the word level and the commitment of my life is not bad or regrettable. It is me. Likewise, I may become angry at seeing a bully picking on a defenseless victim. I may find that the source of my anger, the thing that is inside me, is a healthy sense of justice and an active compassion for the underdogs of this world.

The important thing is the realization that every emotional reaction of ours is telling us something about ourselves. We must learn not to shift responsibility for these reactions to others, preferring to blame them rather than to learn something about ourselves. When I do react emotionally, I know that not everyone would react as I have. Everyone does not have the same stored-up emotions that I have. In dealing simultaneously with many people, there is a great variety of emotional reactions. They are different people, have different needs; they come out of a different past and are seeking different goals. Consequently, their emotional reactions are different because of something inside each of them. The most I ever do is to stimulate these emotions. Similarly, if I want

Every emotional reaction of ours
is telling us something about ourselves.

to know something about myself, my needs, my self-image, my sensitivity, my psychological programming, and my values, then I must listen to and learn from my own emotions.

Human Emotions: The Iceberg Principle

It is estimated that a floating iceberg is only one-tenth visible. Nine-tenths of the ice block remains submerged beneath the surface of the water. A similar estimate has been suggested with regard to human emotions. The part that we are able to see is only about one-tenth of the total reality. The implication of this suggestion is not that people show only one-tenth of their true, recognized feelings to others, but rather that they are themselves consciously aware of only a small part of their own emotions. We hide the bulk of our emotions even from ourselves by the subconscious defense mechanism called repression.

Of course, nonexpression of emotions is very common. Many human emotions, inwardly recognized, are never expressed. For example, "I'll never let her know that I am jealous." There are two basic reasons for this nonexpression of recognized feelings: first, we may doubt that others would understand. They would certainly wonder about us, and possibly would question either our sanity or our integrity. Such doubt invades that sensitive area in us, the center of human behavior and existence: our self-image and consequent self-acceptance-appreciation-celebration. The second possible motive for nonexpression of emotions is even more frightening. We fear that our emotional admissions could be used against us, either thoughtlessly or cruelly. Others might bring it up later, and even if they don't bring it up explicitly, we will always wonder if they are pitying us, afraid of us, or distancing themselves from us. We will wonder if their reactions are a result of the feelings we have confided to them.

Nonexpression is not good, but the repression of emotions into the subconscious is even more self-destructive. While we know that we are hurting when we have repressed our true feelings, we do not know why. We have hidden the source of pain in the "dungeon" of the subconscious. Repressed emotions unfortunately do not die. They refuse to be silenced. They pervasively influence the whole personality and behavior of the repressor. For example, when we repress guilt feelings, we are forever, though we are not aware of it, trying to punish ourselves. We will never allow ourselves success or enjoyment without some punishing qualification. Repressed fears and angers may be "acted out" physically as insomnia, headaches, or ulcers. If such fears and angers had been consciously accepted and reported in detail to another, there would have been no necessity for the sleeplessness, the tension headaches, or ulcers.

The Reasons
for Our Repression

There are three general motives for this emotional repression. We bury undesirable emotions because:

(1) *We have been programmed to do this.* The so-called "parent tapes" of our early indoctrination are constantly replaying their messages in us. Our deepest instincts have been educated in the first five years of our lives by our parents and others who have influenced us. A child from a nondemonstrative family will certainly have a tendency to repress emotions of tenderness and affection. A child who grows up in a constantly fighting family may be very comfortable with the acknowledgment and expression of

anger, but trained to repress gentler emotions such as compassion and remorse.

(2) *We "moralize" emotions.* Depending on our background, we tend to label certain emotions "good" or "bad." For example, it is good to feel grateful but bad to feel angry or jealous. Foolishly but factually, parents often tell their children: "You have *no right* to feel that way," or "You *shouldn't* feel angry; you *ought* to feel sorry for him." For some reason, the one valid emotion that our society has almost universally quarantined out of sight is feeling sorry for oneself, the emotion of self-pity. Indeed, self-pity has become a dirty word.

(3) *We experience a "value conflict."* For example, if "being a man" has become an important part of my identity and self-image, a value upon which I place high premium, certain emotions will almost certainly be considered damaging to this image. I will have to edit my emotions carefully to preserve my masculinity. For the first forty years of my own life, I personally could not admit fear of anyone or anything. At least that is what my head kept thinking and my mouth kept saying. But my poor stomach bore the brunt of my repression. Somehow my intestines did not really believe my head and my mouth. I preferred Tums to the truth.

Sometimes I think that all three of these motives for repression can be reduced to one simple motive. What I need in order to go on living is self-acceptance-esteem-appreciation-celebration. I have tried to build up some kind of structure that will allow me this needed self-acceptance. I admit that it is like a house of match sticks. I must protect it from all threats: those that come from within as well as those that come from the outside. Emotions arising from within, if they are judged incompatible with self-acceptance, might endanger the precarious, leaning tower of my self-image. I cannot have that. So I have headaches, allergies, ulcers, virus colds, and spastic parts. Buried emotions are like rejected people; they make us pay a high price for having rejected them. Hell hath no fury like that of a scorned emotion.

The Real Loss
of Lost Emotions

Lost or repressed emotions are not really lost. They continue, in one way or another, to remind us that we really didn't get away with the attempted rejection. Aside from this built-in system of painful sanctions, the essential tragedy of repression is that the whole process of human growth is shut down, at least temporarily. Psychologists call this state "fixation," an arrest of growth and development.

I think that this truth about living has been very dramatically illustrated in the research and writing on death and dying by Dr. Elisabeth Kübler-Ross. What the doctor writes about acceptance of death seems to apply equally well to the acceptance of self and the realities of life. Both acts of acceptance (of death and self) require a serial process of emotional reactions. And each of these emotional steps must be fully experienced for the successful completion of the process.

Dr. Kübler-Ross theorizes that terminal patients, after being informed of approaching death, rarely if ever are capable of immediate and full acceptance. They must pass through various stages, the first of which is a stage of *denial:* "No, not me." Unable to cope with the fact that life for them will soon be over, they erase the handwriting on the wall by denial.

Following the stage of denial, according to the research of Kübler-Ross, the patients enter into a period of *anger, rage, and indignation.* "Not me" becomes "Why me?" Their anger is often by displacement directed to hospital personnel. "This food is cold . . . That injection hurts" is really saying: "You are going to live. I am going to die. You are going to raise your children and see your grandchildren. I am going to be taken from my children before they are raised." The hospital staff is resented, not for any of the pretended reasons, but because they are healthy and have the promise of continued life.

In the third stage, this edge of anger and rage mellows into a stance of *bargaining.* The "Why me?" becomes "Yes me, but maybe . . ." The bargaining overtures are made to the doctor—"I'll never smoke again!" or even to God—"I'll go to church every Sunday!"

The fourth stage is one of *resignation in depression:* "Yes me, damn it! I'm going to die, and I am resigned to the inevitable fact, but I don't want to die." Externally, the patients go through a period of silent reluctance and sadness, but they are at this stage confronting the fact of death more realistically. Of course, the final stage in the process is one of peaceful *acceptance.* "I am going to die. My life's work is over. I am ready." This final stage of acceptance is characterized externally in quiet, silent prayer.

The significant and relevant thing is what Dr. Kübler-Ross says about the *process* of these stages. Like steps of a ladder, each one must be negotiated separately and usually in order. Kübler-Ross warns that if anyone interferes with the process, trying to keep a patient in one stage, like denial, or move the patient from one to another before she or he is ready, the whole process moving toward acceptance is automatically shut down. Often families want a person who is dying to play the "denial game." Ninety-five per cent of all such patients are not really fooled. However, the family will not let them go on into the more difficult emotions partly because they want to spare the dying patients but also because they don't know how to handle and live with these more difficult emotions. Often we tell people not to cry in order to spare ourselves the necessity of having to cope with tears.

Dr. Kübler-Ross relates that often a well-intentioned chaplain can attempt to move a person from emotions of resistance, like anger and indignation, into the theologically compatible emotion of acceptance. He waves over the head of the dying person the magic wand: "It is God's will." If the dying person tries to alter his or her emotional patterns to accommodate the chaplain, the process is prematurely over. The anger and indignation must be acknowledged and expended before full acceptance becomes a possibility.

Dr. Kübler-Ross tells of her own dealing with a dying woman who asked if there was a "screaming room" in the hospital. When Dr. Kübler-Ross told her that there was a chapel where she could pray, the woman angrily replied: "If I felt like praying, I would have asked for the chapel. I want to scream!"

The point of reviewing Dr. Kübler-Ross's research is to suggest that there are not only essential, emotional stages on the way to the acceptance of death, but also a comparable process of stages on the way to the acceptance of self and life. Like the dying, those who would live fully must go through periods of denial, simply refusing to accept themselves as they are, by denying the facts of their own unique human condition. There are also periods of anger and bargaining, and a sad resignation. But if those who love them will stand by, holding out their own acceptance, without any attempt at emotional manipulation, the process will probably have a happy conclusion. The penalty for intrusion and emotional coercion in this self-acceptance process is the same as in the death-acceptance process: fixation, incompletion. The whole process will shut down. Like dust swept under a rug, the rejected emotions will be driven into the labyrinths of the subconscious. However, the price will be extremely high. We must learn to welcome in ourselves and in others the fact of this emotional process and all the feelings that are a part of it. Each emotion is saying something, leading us somewhere.

The real loss of lost emotions is the loss of growth and ultimately the loss of that which is the central need of every human being: realistic self-acceptance, self-esteem, self-appreciation, and self-celebration.

Locating Lost Emotions

Recovering our buried emotions is absolutely essential to human growth. To the extent that we repress, we lose contact with ourselves. We get lost behind our masks and security operations.

At the risk of oversimplification, I would like to suggest that if you really want to listen to your emotions, they will speak to you. Whenever you are ready to stop telling your emotions what they should be, they will tell you what they really are. The discoverer of the subconscious, Sigmund Freud, says that all repressed emotions are constantly trying to break back into consciousness. As a result, according to Dr. Freud, we have to practice "reaction formation," or some other means of continued repression. "Reaction formation" means that we have to keep acting in a manner opposed to the emotions that are being repressed. For example, we assume a brave set of external mannerisms to compensate for the fear we are repressing. Since repressed emotions are trying to surface, they can be kept repressed only with some effort of this kind.

So the first thing we should do is to sit quietly and take a mental, emotional inventory. Do you really want to know what's buried in you? If a doctor offered to give you truth serum and then videotape all your answers to some searching questions, would you be eager or reluctant to volunteer? Would you be ready to revise the suppositions that you have made about yourself? Would you be ready to admit that some of your alleged motives for action are really phony? Could you face the fact that you are perhaps displacing emotions on innocent bystanders, blaming others for things you cannot accept in yourself? These are all possibilities, and they must be considered. How much do you love the truth and really want to know yourself?

My own answer is that I do want the full prescription but in small doses. I want the full story, but I think I can take only one chapter at a time. I don't feel strong enough because I don't love myself enough to face everything at once. I think that this is why so many people have been pushed over the brink into insanity by mind-expanding drugs. As one young experimenter said after his "bad trip": "I've been to places inside myself where no one should ever go."

Fortunately, nature is more kind and merciful than narcotics. The subconscious divulges its contents gradually in proportion to our strengths. To the extent that we love, esteem, appreciate, and celebrate our reality we become more flexible with the contents of the subconscious and more open to this whole process. To the extent that we are aware of our possession of many desirable qualities we will have the confidence to face what may seem undesirable. So a willingness and even eagerness to know the truth is the point of departure for everyone. Only the full acceptance of the full truth can lead us to the fullness of life. Now for more specific methods.

Free Association in Friendship

Psychoanalysis is the process of dredging the subconscious of its repressed contents and conflicts. In analysis the "fundamental technique" is called free association. The patient is directed not to prepare a report for the analyst, but to report spontaneously anything and everything that comes to mind, even though it may seem illogical or irrelevant. The patient tries to become as free as possible from external stimuli and conscious control. He or she is encouraged to verbalize whatever comes to mind, whatever feelings arise, and whatever memories are recalled. The supposition is that all the burdens of the subconscious want release, and in the atmosphere of free association the patient is saying "yes," giving free rein to all the repressed impulses, emotions, ideas, and experiences that have been subconsciously buried but reflected in crippling attitudes and behavior.

There are many excellent analysts ready to help us with the process, which is long and expensive. Somehow I believe that this very process also can be achieved in true friendship. However, I think that relatively few "friendships" accomplish the kind of freeing, spontaneous, and reassuring atmosphere necessary for the release of these subconscious burdens. But the best advice is still, and will always be, to find a good friend and confidant. Find a person who accepts you in your ups and downs, and who will not hold you responsible to the logistical rules of coherence in your communication. And if this person becomes more manipulative than liberative, speak up. Convince your friend that his or her greatest contribution and assistance will be to help you find and face the truth about yourself.

Psychosomatic
Self-analysis

There is another popular method of locating lost emotions, a technique evolved by Dr. Eugene T. Gendlin. Like all other therapeutic techniques, it requires practice. I have found this to be of great help to myself on many occasions. The supposition of this theory is that people begin to make progress, sick people get better and healthy people become healthier, when they get in touch with their emotions and the reasons for those emotions. This, I think, is an almost universal supposition of modern psychology. Gendlin's theory also supposes that all repressed emotions somehow are "acted out" in physical symptoms, the most common of which are tension, fatigue, headaches, and respiratory or intestinal discomfort. In the technique suggested, one begins with a conscious awareness of one's physical reactions, which are really repressed emotions translated into physical symptoms. The body is the biological computer which records everything that is going on in us.

By an interior dialogue with the body, the reconversion of the physical reaction into the original emotion is welcomed. To verbalize this interior act, the person would say something like this to a headache: "You first came to me as an emotion, but I didn't want to experience you, so you have become a headache. Now I want you to come back as a feeling. I will have you. I will be willing to feel whatever emotion you are." Under such invitation, the physical reaction is slowly changed back into a feeling—a feeling of fear, anger, or whatever. It may be accompanied by a fantasy like sinking in quicksand or groping through a forest.

When the feeling has become relatively clear, the person then explores the possible reasons for such a feeling. He or she will probably have to experiment with various hypotheses. But when the true emotion and the full reason for it are finally located, the physical symptom will begin immediately to diminish and will disappear. The beauty of this system is that there is a built-in test of success: the disappearance of the physical reaction.

Perhaps an example from my own experience will help clarify this explanation. Several years ago I drove to Canada to make a preached retreat of one week. The preacher had been highly recommended, and my first impressions were extremely favorable. Then anger began to build in me. I felt very irritable and noticed a growing aversion for both the retreat director and the other people in attendance. After four or five days, I was tense and troubled. I knew that I was repressing and displacing my emotions. What I saw, however, was only the tip of the iceberg. So I lay quietly on my bed, listening attentively to my own body with its tensions, the dull ache of my muscles, the slight pain in my neck and shoulders.

I invited these physical discomforts to reconvert into the emotions I had rejected. I invited those emotions to arise in me. If Freud is right that we must strain to keep repressed emotions repressed, relaxing in this way can be an important part of the process of recovering our lost emotions, but the essential thing is always the attitude of openness.

Out of somewhere deep inside me came not anger—my anger was like most anger, only a cover-up—but a bleak and bitter sense of personal failure. It was clear after a matter of minutes that this was the true emotion I had repressed. This strange sense of failure became very strong in me. Then I began the final phase of this method of self-analysis, letting my mind range over various hypotheses. Could it be this . . . that? Then in a moment of sudden insight, it became clear.

The retreat master was a saintly, loving, dedicated man. He appeared to be all the things that I wanted most to be but had not in fact become. Rather than accept my emotions of failure, stimulated by contact with such a holy man, I repressed them, and worked at the repression by a kind of reaction formation: feeling hostile toward the very man that I so deeply admired. At the moment I was willing to accept the feelings of my failure and acknowledge the reasons for those feelings, all tension drained out of me and, of course, there was no further need to displace my true feelings. I enjoyed a deep peace, and most of all I had learned something about myself, my deepest desire and my deepest pain.

A Popular Method: Transactional Analysis

Transactional analysis originated with the late California psychiatrist Eric Berne as a method of "group" therapy. Berne believed that the starting point in therapy should be the transactions or interactions among the people in the group. Analysis of these transactions, he felt, would reveal the hidden or repressed emotional influences on behavior.

The man responsible for making T.A. available to the average person is a disciple of Berne, Dr. Thomas Harris, especially through his best-selling *I'm OK—You're OK.* Harris proposes T.A. as a method of acknowledging repressed emotional factors in behavior, admitting that we are very profoundly influenced by others very early in life, but insisting that we are free and responsible for what we will become.

It is true that we are largely the product of past experience. Every event of our lives and the emotional reactions accompanying those events are recorded in our brains, in every muscle, cell, and fiber of our being. So these events, and especially the feelings we associated with them, are always replaying inside us, but most of this remains subconscious. We are rarely aware—without practice at T.A.—of the connection between our reaction to present events and this backlog of past experience and feeling. For example, I may have a hostile attitude or perhaps a fearful attitude toward all authority figures because my parents were domineering; but I may never be aware of this connection.

T.A. is a practical way of understanding these connections, of relating past emotional reactions, still lingering in us, to present experience and behavior. If we are willing to act against inhibiting or crippling feelings, we will be able to change our habits of behavior, and consequently the course of our lives. But the first necessity is to get to those buried feelings, and the starting point for this is to observe ourselves in action, in the transactions of every day.

Each of our interactions with another is a "transaction." In the normal transaction, one party offers a "stimulus," in word or gesture, and the other reacts with a transactional "response." The whole point of analyzing the transaction is to recognize and evaluate the underlying emotional influences of both the stimulus and the response.

Let us take an example. Transaction: Someone pays you a compliment. How do you react? Do you get wordy? Do you stammer? Do you change the topic? Do you blush or look away? Under your response lies an emotional backlog. What is this feeling under your reaction? Did you feel glad to be recognized? Were you happy but embarrassed to show it? The practice of T.A. promotes conscious awareness of such connections, so that we can effectively redirect our lives. Unless we see and act against crippling emotions, our futures will be merely a playing out of previous programming. This is the most exciting feature of T.A. for most people: the hope that we can change. We can "move out of the tyranny of the past . . . to exercise self-direction and freedom of choice."

The theory of T.A. begins with the supposition of Alfred Adler that all human beings are afflicted with deep feelings of inferiority, a feeling of being "not OK." Harris believes that most people never fulfill their human promise and potential because they remain perpetually helpless children overwhelmed by a sense of inferiority. The feeling of being OK does not imply that people have risen above all their faults and emotional problems. It merely implies that they refuse to be paralyzed by them. They are determined to accept themselves as they are but also to assume more and more control of their lives.

According to Harris, there are four basic attitudes or positions which we take with regard to ourselves and others:

1 I'm not OK—You're OK.
2 I'm not OK—You're not OK.
3 I'm OK—You're not OK.
4 I'm OK—You're OK.

The first position is the universal position of every child at age five. Children at this age have been almost totally dependent on others and so their deepest feelings at this time are usually feelings of dependence and inadequacy, and a strong need for approval from those upon whom they depend. Harris says that although the words stick in his throat, there is no such thing as a happy childhood. The messages that have been recorded in us during these first five years all emphasize our dependency, inadequacy, and deficiency. Some parental messages are affirming, but most of them are not. And so the first conclusion we come to about ourselves is: I'm not OK. I can't do anything right. And the first question we ask is: What can I possibly do to please you?

The extent to which we have remained stuck in this first position of not being OK is indicated by definite symptoms: We feel inferior in dealing with others. We need the approval of others very badly. We have problems with jealousy. We have an insatiable ambition to be as OK as others, as wealthy, intelligent, or good-looking as others are. This ambition is usually directed to those who are close and important to us. To the extent that we have not moved out of this first position, we tend to live in a fantasy world, to experience hostility, depression, and even despair.

If a child is not given sufficient recognition and love ("stroking"), position one becomes position two very early in life. The second position is basically one of withdrawal because positive strokes of praise and affection have been withheld. The inner attitude is: "I'm not OK, but you're not OK either because you have hurt me. You have not loved me." And a child who is severely mistreated ("brutal stroking") is likely to move into the third position, a vindictive attitude: "I'm OK and you're not OK, and it's going to cost you." In the attitude of Papillon: "You dished out all you had, and I'm still alive."

All of these first three positions are unconsciously adopted. They are based on feelings that are largely subconscious. The fourth position by contrast is a conscious decision and choice, based on thought, faith, and action.

To make this choice effectively, we must come to a realization that there are three components in our personalities. As we have all felt at times, we are not really one but three persons all wrapped up in one. Sometimes we behave as an *adult*; we are rational and mature, capable of decisions and in conscious control of our lives. At other times we seem to regress to childish or even infantile reactions, demanding immediate gratification and "our own way." There is also a wholesome side of this *child* in us; we like swings, running along a beach, picking flowers, and so on. Finally, there are times when we are a living replica of our *parents,* a living composite of all their messages recorded and always playing in us.

In the terminology of T.A., these are the three familiar "ego states": Parent—Adult—Child. They are in all of us, and we vacillate from one to another, usually without awareness unless we have worked at T.A. It is this precise awareness that T.A. would teach. Both Berne and Harris insist that we can learn to recognize the ego state in a given transaction by detectable changes in our manners, gestures, appearance, and in the very words we choose, our vocal inflections, and so forth.

The Parent. The Parent in us is a composite of all the messages recorded in us during the first five years of life. We are acting in the ego state of Parent when our behavior is determined by these messages, which are fixed, unchanging, dogmatic. They are for the most part critical, restricting, controlling, and inhibiting. Some of these messages may well be supportive and affirming.

The Adult. The Adult is mature, decisive, flexible. While the Parent and Child are relatively fixed states in which there can be little modification after childhood, the Adult is where we are open to change and growth. All hope for a different and better existence resides here. The Adult in us listens to, reviews, and evaluates those fixed parental messages, decides what to act upon and what to act against. From ages one to five we are incapable of evaluating what is said and done to us. We record everything as "the truth." The function of Adult, with regard to the Parent, is to reevaluate those experiences and messages. The Adult also listens to the emotional hurts and enthusiasms of the Child, and allows or disallows the Child's whims in the light of mature values and rational decisions. It is the Adult ego state that must dominate the personality, remain in the ascendancy, or, in the language of T.A., "get plugged in."

The Child. The Child in us is spontaneous, lively, creative, motivated by feelings. All emotional reactions from ecstasy to despair are stored here. The hurts acquired in our early relationships are also recorded here. The Child in us tends to be primitive and self-depreciating yet capable of excitement, wonder, and enthusiasm. The Child can bring to our whole personalities all the happiness that a lively child brings to a family group. So the Adult in us should allow the Child to express joy and enthusiasm.

The genius of T.A. in practice is to learn how to recognize each of these states in ourselves. Parents are dogmatic and rigid. They use words like "should . . . shouldn't . . . always . . . never . . . once and for all . . . If I were you . . . nonsense . . . It must be done this way . . ." The tone of voice is commanding or condescending. The facial expressions are judgmental, concerned, shocked, righteous. The Child is found in such expressions as quivering lips, pouting, whining, temper tantrums, downcast eyes, sobbing, jumping up and down, giggling, squirming, shrieking. The Child's vocabulary is punctuated by "I want . . . I need . . . I wish . . . I won't . . . I can't . . . I guess . . . I don't care . . . I don't know . . . I feel . . . I am going to . . . Give me . . ."

Once we have become facile at getting in touch with our ego states, we have arrived at the possibility of emancipating the Adult, of putting the Adult in charge. We are then neither controlled by the narrow and fixed positions of the Parent nor by the insatiable needs of the Child. Life is governed gently but forcibly by reason, although at the same time we happily love and recognize that which is good in the Parent and in the Child. We welcome the boundaries and wisdom of the Parent, the wonder, creativity, and enthusiasm of the Child.

We can become proficient at one of the methods recommended. With practice and perseverance we can learn to recognize the emotional forces that underlie our behavior. We can practice the needed self-discipline in acting against our emotions when those emotions would be crippling and destructive. With the help of God and those who love us, we can rewrite our "life script." We can then move realistically toward self-acceptance, self-esteem, self-appreciation, and self-celebration.

They were brother priests and brother Jesuits. They had for many years experienced a rich and rewarding friendship. The two had trudged together through the wilderness of the long seminary training. When one had a special need—for time, a listening ear, or whatever, the other had always been there.

The friendship was ended abruptly in tragedy and death. One of the two friends was hit by a car and killed in front of the residence where the two priests lived with their community.

When the other was informed that his friend lay dead on the street, he went running, cut through the cordon of onlookers and police, and knelt at the side of his old friend. He gently cradled the dead man's head on his arm, and before all those gaping people, he blurted out:

"Don't die! You can't die! I never told you that I loved you."

The daily bread of dialogue

As we have defined dialogue it centers around the communication or sharing of emotions. The purpose of this dialogue is to enable the partners to come to a deeper knowledge, understanding, and fuller acceptance of each other in love. Dialogue is always moving toward encounter, toward the mutual experience of each other's person through this sharing of feelings. It is not for solving problems, exchanging ideas, making choices, giving and receiving advice, laying plans, or reasoning things out. All these belong to discussion. Effective dialogue is an absolutely essential prerequisite for fruitful discussions.

The assumption of dialogue is that all feelings are very natural reactions that are the result of countless influences spaced out over the whole of one's life. They can be stimulated by another but never caused by another. They are in us, and most probably have been stored in us since early childhood. They represent no danger and have absolutely no moral implications. We never need a reason, excuse, or explanation for the way we feel. It's okay to feel whatever we feel. The only real danger is to ignore, deny, or refuse to report our feelings. The repression or nonexpression of emotions leads to a generalized distortion of the whole human personality and to a great variety of painful symptoms.

There is absolutely no place in dialogue for arguing. Dialogue is essentially an exchange of feelings and there cannot be any argument over the way a person feels. There is room for argumentation in discussion, and couples must pass eventually from dialogue into discussion. We have to know how the other thinks, what the other prefers, so that we can make plans and decisions together. Problems requiring discussion constantly enter our lives, and we must deal with them together. However, we must be sure that dialogue is really completed before discussion begins.

Finally, true dialogue is characterized by a sense of collaboration, not competition. If there is a sense of contest, whatever is going on isn't dialogue. Dialogue is the simple exchange of feelings without any attempt to analyze, rationalize, or assign responsibility for those feelings. Therefore, a partner who thinks that the other partner should not feel a certain way has really missed the whole point. She or he is probably rejecting the whole idea of dialogue and probably rejecting his or her partner as well. However, if the couple is discovering a fresh beauty and new depths of goodness in each other's person, if they have a growing feeling of getting to know each other, they are succeeding in the art of dialogue.

Motives for Dialogue

Many years ago I read a book on public speaking. The first chapter was entitled "Never Try to Be a Better Speaker Than You Are a Person Because Your Audience Will Know." It was reminiscent of Quintillian's definition of a good speaker: a good person who speaks well. The obvious implication is that our motives usually show through in spite of our attempts to camouflage them. We have all felt and been misunderstood at times, but over the long haul, the intuitions of others about our motivation are usually accurate if incomplete. People attempting dialogue should listen sensitively, therefore, to their motives. I suggest that there are three possibilities to be given special consideration.

Ventilation. When we ventilate a room, we air it out. We rid it of stale air or odors. Emotions, too, can accumulate inside us to the extent that we feel a need to ventilate them, to get them "off our chest." There may be occasional moments when this is necessary, but the fewer they are, the better the dialogue and relationship will be.

Ventilation is essentially egocentric. I want to feel better, so I am using you as a garbage dump for my emotional refuse. The occasional necessity for such ventilation is understandable, but nobody wants to be a habitual garbage dump or crying towel. Pouring out my emotional troubles to you so that I can feel better is self-centered. If it becomes a habit, a self-centered person develops, and such a person has little capacity for dialogue or love.

Manipulation. The second possible motive to be considered is manipulation. Love, we have said, is essentially freeing. Love asks only: "What can I do for you? What do you need me to be?" The unexpressed question in manipulation is exactly the opposite: "What can you do for me?" Manipulation is a sleight-of-hand way of pressuring another into fulfilling my needs. Now, obviously there are going to be times when I need you to help me, to stay with me, to listen to me. I should feel free to ask you without fear of rejection.

Manipulation, however, as a motive for dialogue, implies that I report and describe my feelings to another so that the other will do something about them. As a manipulator I make the other feel responsible for my emotions. For example, I can tell you that I am lonely. It is simply a fact that I am going through a period of loneliness, and I want you to know that because I want you to know me. Or I can tell you in such a way that I clearly imply your responsibility to fill the void of my loneliness. By subtle innuendos of voice, facial expression, and so on, I make you feel the necessity to fulfill my needs. I am, by indirection and suggestion, using emotional leverage on you to get you to solve my problems.

There are no ways to uncover ventilation or manipulation as hidden motives in dialogue. We must remember, however, that if we fall into the temptation, we can protest our innocence to others and even convince ourselves, but others will know. Never try to be a better speaker than you are a person because your audience will know. When we are motivated habitually by the desire to ventilate or manipulate, we turn people into things. We value and deal with them only in terms of their value, function, and usefulness to us. When partners in dialogue do this, they degrade themselves and destroy their relationship. They soon drift off into monologue, and that is the way to alienation, to loneliness, to nowhere.

Communication. The only motive from which true dialogue can result is the desire for communication. We have said that communication means sharing, and that we share our real selves when we share our feelings. Consequently, the only valid motive for dialogue is this desire to give to another the most precious thing I can give: myself in self-disclosure, in the transparency achieved in dialogue.

Note: I'm sure you have felt at times, as I have, that others are not really interested in you. Not even those who supposedly love us and whom we supposedly love seem very interested in listening to us. I have certainly known many wives who feel this way about their husbands and many husbands who feel this way about their wives. The same thing is often reported to me by young people whose parents supposedly aren't interested in them. I really think that many or most of these cases can be explained by the fact that the "put off" party was using one of the first two motives for self-disclosure: either ventilation or manipulation. I know from my own experience that I get uncomfortable when I feel that I am being used or manipulated by another. I begin looking at the clock, looking for a way out. Human nature is essentially gregarious. The law of togetherness is written upon our hearts. However, this desire to know and to be known does not include the wish to be a garbage dump or a problem solver. We don't want to feel "used."

Trust Is a Choice

Anyone who has ever contemplated taking the risk of emotional transparency has also asked: Can I trust you? How far can I trust you? Will you understand or will you reject my feelings? Would you laugh at me or pity me? The usual procedure is to play swimmer, testing the temperature of the water, one toe at a time. Unfortunately, most of us decide to wait until we are sure and so never get into the healing waters of dialogue.

Waiting until we have an absolute guarantee of trust reminds me of a story I once heard. It seems that the mother of a young boy told his friends who had invited the boy to go swimming: "I am not going to allow Michael to go into the water until he learns to swim." Obviously, the only way to learn to swim is by getting into the water. Likewise the only way one learns to trust is to trust.

Dialogue cannot be delayed. The court can't bring in a verdict until the trial is held. And so dialogue demands an act of the will: I am going to trust you. I can't be sure. Perhaps you will disappoint me. But I am going to risk, to take a chance, to open my most sensitive feelings to you because I want to give you this, my most valuable gift . . . because I love you. Because I love you I am going to give you, as my first gift, my trust.

The Myth of Privacy

One of our strongest needs, which can easily become a neurotic preoccupation, is the need to feel safe. And so most of us like to have a room of our own with selected signs for the door, like: PRIVATE—DO NOT TRESPASS or DO NOT DISTURB. We want a place of safety, barricaded against the invasion of others with their probing questions and inquisitive desire to know all about us. There is no nakedness more painful than psychological nakedness. Out of this need to feel safe and protected from the searching eyes of another grows a myth that everyone needs a private retreat where no one else can enter. It sounds good; it looks good; most people probably believe it. It is, nevertheless, a misleading myth: something we wish were true but is really not true.

Human nature is essentially gregarious.

Rather than a place reserved exclusively for self, what we really need is to have someone (a total confidant) know us completely and some others (close friends) know us very deeply. The pockets of privacy that we create for a place to run where no one can follow are death to the kind of human intimacy so necessary to the fullness of human life.

First of all, and it has become a cliché by now, I can know only so much of myself as I have the courage to confide to you. If I can feel totally free with you in a place cleared of "do not trespass" signs, I will no doubt go with the assurance of your companionship into places inside myself I could never have known existed. I will go into places I could never have gone alone. I need your hand in mine and the assurance of your committed and unconditional love even to attempt honesty about myself.

Second, your love will be effective only to the extent that I confide myself to you. When you say in one of the many ways that love is expressed that you love me, I will want to believe that you really know me. To the extent that I have hidden myself from you, the meaning of your love will be diminished. I will forever fear that you love only the part of me that I have let you know, and that if you knew the real me, all of me, you would not love me. Love follows upon knowledge, and so you can love me only to the extent that I let you know me.

It is true that, in all communication, kindness without honesty is sentimentality, but it is likewise true that honesty without kindness is cruelty. The genius of communication is the ability to be both totally honest and totally kind at the same time. It is one of the stern canons of dialogue that emotions should be reported at the time they are experienced and to the person to whom those emotions are related. Still, kindness should have much to say about the manner of communication.

But what about things that are not strictly emotions, but rather old "closed rooms" which have been a part of our human estate for a long time and which are the cluster point of many emotions? Oftentimes these "secrets of the past" have a definite effect on one's self-image and behavior. Let us say, for example, that there is a secret shame, a humiliating failure from my past, or a neurotic inclination which I have never exposed to anyone. Perhaps if I told my partner in dialogue, he or she would think differently of me and might even begin to suspect me or my normalcy.

Some say that you cannot be totally open and honest with those you love. It would destroy them. These people say that we need only to be *real* in the part of ourselves that we do reveal. For the reasons given earlier I do not believe this. I do believe that these communications, which are not strictly and only emotions but which can have deep emotional implications, should be prudently timed.

Each person must make a fundamental judgment about the stability, the depth of understanding and acceptance in the relationship involved. The presumption is that these communications should be made now, or if that would seem imprudent, the revelation should be made at some time in the future when the necessary depth of understanding and acceptance has been achieved. Permanent withholding will always create a permanent deficiency in the relationship, an obstacle to the love that could have been.

No Judgments Allowed

Of all the threats to successful dialogue, the one to be most carefully avoided is the intrusion of judgments, either about oneself or about one's partner in dialogue. We have said that no one can cause our emotions, but can only stimulate emotions that are already in us. The most common way that judgments enter into and ruin dialogue is through the door of my believing that you have caused my emotions. Or I might think that there is such an obvious connection between your action and my emotion that "anyone would have reacted as I did." Both reactions are based on judgments and both judgments have to be false.

For example, we agreed to meet at a certain time and in a certain place. You arrive one half hour late. I am angry. I should tell you this as a simple fact, implying only that there is something in me that reacts angrily when I am left waiting. But think of the possible judgmental accusations that could enter into my words, voice inflection, or facial expressions.

"You could have been on time."
"You acted inconsiderately."
"You didn't care about my feelings."
"You don't really love me."
"You're always late."
"You're very selfish."
"You did this to hurt me or to get even with me."
"This is why you have no friends."
"You don't think ahead."
"Anyone else would have left on time to get here."

Notice that all these judgments obviously put me into a superior position in our dialogue. This is the kind of "presumed advantage" that has no place in true dialogue. You might have emotions of your own, like embarrassment or frustration; but when I decide that righteousness is mine and suppose a privileged and superior position, it becomes obvious that my emotions must be handled, not yours. Judgments are death to true dialogue. Furthermore, the kind of judgments we are tempted to make usually involve a kind of indirect, destructive criticism that is fatal to self-acceptance, self-appreciation, and self-celebration. And when they have gone, love has been lost.

How to Speak
in Dialogue

The disposition to dialogue is very briefly this: I want you to know me. I come to dialogue in search of mutual understanding, not in pursuit of victory. I want to share my most precious possession, myself, with you. Emotional warning flags are fluttering all over the place, telling me that this is risky business. Of course, I know this. But I want to take this risk for you because I love you and want to make this an act of love. I know that there is no gift of love without this gift of myself through self-disclosure.

I know also that I am *asking* through this self-revelation. I am asking first for your understanding and acceptance. I am also inviting you to reciprocate, to share yourself with me. You, too, will probably experience instinctively a sense of my taking this risk. It may be that my taking this risk for you will empower you to take a risk for me. Whenever you are ready for that risk, I will be here for you. Do not feel that you must respond to me on my terms or at my time. Love is freeing, and so my love for you must always leave you free to respond in your own way and at your own time.

The essence of risk is this: I have needs. When I reveal my feelings to you, you will know this. I will have to tell you about my loneliness, my discouragement, my self-pity, my fears in facing life. The myth of my self-sufficiency will be exploded. I will have no more of the old facades of nonchalance or bravado to hide behind. The pretense of my self-sufficiency was both ego-supportive and ego-defensive. But it has kept you from knowing the real me. So I am going to sacrifice it for you because I want you to know the true me. When I have left all my other games, the protection of my sham and pretense, and when I have left myself naked before you, will you stay with me and clothe me with the gentle garments of your understanding?

It is relatively easy to see why this risk is necessary in a love relationship. Love, we said, asks the question: "What do you need me to be, to do?" If I am not willing to acknowledge my needs honestly and openly, then there is no place in my life for your love. You could never feel that you are really important to me. You would eventually leave me. You would never want to be just another pair of clapping hands in my audience.

So I come to you in dialogue, wanting you to know me and willing to take this essential risk of transparency in the revelation of my needs. In doing so I must remember that what I will tell you is uniquely mine to offer you. The heart of my revelation will not be my thoughts. Everyone could know every thought I ever had and not really know me. I must share with you my deepest feelings. When I give you from the store of my thoughts, opinions, and preferences, I somehow know that I am giving of my excess. When I give you my deepest feelings, I am giving you my very substance. I am giving you the real meaning of me.

It should also be remembered that each person feels in a unique way the emotions common to everyone. My feelings of depression or hurt are not yours. It is also true that each person reacts physically in a different way. Some people develop strong bodily sensations under the influence of certain emotions, while others react to the same feelings by turning numb and freezing. Likewise, social reactions are different. When some people are hurt, they want only to be

left alone, while others instin
whom they can describe their h\

So speakers in dialogue must
uniquely theirs, and as graphicall
When Adlai Stevenson II lost in his
he said he felt like a little boy who l
toe. "It hurts too much to laugh, but   ⊃ſ
course, having Stevenson's gift of eloq\   ∪ help, but
I have to work with what I've got, ev⌐⌐ ıſ everything I say
doesn't become immediately memorable or quotable. I can
still feel like "there's a funeral going on in my heart . . . I feel
like a pebble on a beach . . . I feel like a cancelled stamp in
the great post office of life."

In order to achieve the quality of emotional description
which will enable the listener to experience the same
emotions, the speaker must first try to feel his or her emotions
as deeply as possible. Most people don't spend enough time
allowing their emotions to surface and sensitively listening
to them. We are usually tempted to rush off into some
distraction or into an intellectual analysis of the feelings. Only
rarely do we fully and consciously have our emotions. It is
obvious that I can communicate to you only what I have been
willing to hear inside myself. If I do not listen carefully to my
own fully emerged emotions, the sounds will be vague and
my descriptions to you will be equally vague. And vague
sounds do not lead to the profound sharing of feelings, to the
peak experiences of communication which transform and
deepen a love relationship.

I must, as a speaker in dialogue, be so vivid that you can
feel and live my emotions. I don't want to tell you about that
emotion; I want to transplant it into you. I want you to taste
my bitterness, to wander around in the debris of my failure,
to feel the pumping adrenalin of my spectacular success. In

am not telling you abstract truths about me, but
que truth of me at this moment in my life. Remember
at it is my feelings that individuate me, that make me
different from everyone else. And the feelings I am having right
now make me different from what I have ever been or will
ever become. I want to share with you this unrepeatable
moment in my personal history.

Lastly, some kind of context for the emotional content of
dialogue should be a part of the speaker's responsibility. The
total communication might be visualized as having three parts:
(1) a brief description of yourself in terms of physical,
subjective influences that might be affecting your emotional
state (for example, "I am very tired . . . I am on a strict diet
. . . I quit smoking a week ago"), (2) the specific events of
the day that stimulated the emotions to be revealed (for
example, "I was refused the raise I asked for . . . I saw this
movie and . . . I failed my chemistry exam . . . You told me
you were too busy and couldn't help me"), (3) the emotions
themselves.

The first two parts can be handled very briefly, as their only
function is to provide some kind of context and perspective
for the emotions, which are the heart of dialogue.

How to Listen
in Dialogue

God gave us two ears but only one mouth, which the Irish
have interpreted as a divine suggestion that we should listen
twice as much as we talk. Whether this be true or not, 50
percent of our personal success at dialogue is determined by
how well we listen. Paul Tournier talks of the "dialogues of
the deaf, in which no one really listens." If people do not listen,

it is either because they are not interested or because they feel threatened by what they might hear. Consequently, real dialogue and real listening belong to a world of understanding and love. Real dialogue can occur only here. Any suggestion or feeling of competition, of being in a win-lose contest is a certain sign that dialogue has not been achieved. Reuel Howe, in his book *The Miracle of Dialogue,* says that everyone "is a potential adversary, even those we love. Only through dialogue are we saved from this enmity toward one another. Dialogue is to love what blood is to the body."

And so the special virtue of the listener in dialogue is empathy. The true listener wants only to understand, to arrive at that moment when he or she can honestly say: "I hear you. I am sharing your feelings. I am feeling them with you." To be true listeners we must be available, be called out of ourselves in an act of listening. We are not afraid of what we will hear because all we seek is mutual understanding, not victory. We have no ready suggestions, no facile solutions, and no pink pills of pity ready to dispense. We don't interrupt except when necessary for our own better understanding. We don't think about our response while the other is talking. And when the emotions of the speaker take a clear shape, we accept them into ourselves. We do not merely tolerate them with a condescending: I will allow you to have that emotion.

Basically, the true listener acknowledges and respects otherness in the speaker. Many people carry around inside themselves a little checklist with which to run others through the test of conformity. Such people prefer the whole world to be a carbon copy of themselves. The classical figure of the nonlistener is Archie Bunker, the television character. Archie talks at people, not to them or with them. He has certain prepared answers on all topics and for all questions. He is a living portrait of the closed mind. He either knows it, or it is not important. Such a person does not have to listen.

We laugh at Archie. He reminds us of somebody we know. But if we are starkly honest with ourselves, we will be able to admit that there is inside each of us a little Archie Bunker who really doesn't listen. He is safe and satisfied where he is. Other people are his pawns, to be manipulated into a position where they can best serve him.

Listening in dialogue is listening more to meanings than to words. It is listening with the heart more than with the head. Dialogue itself is more of a heart trip than a head trip. Such listening is a pondering rather than a quibbling over the meaning of words. In true listening we reach behind the words, see through them, to find the person who is being revealed. Listening is a searching to find the treasure of the true person, as revealed verbally and nonverbally. There is the semantic problem, of course. The same words bear a different connotation for you than they do for me. Consequently, I can never tell you *what you said,* but only *what I heard.* I will have to rephrase what you have said, and check it out with you to make sure that what left your mind and heart arrived in my mind and heart intact and without serious distortion.

Gabriel Marcel says that "presence and availability" are the essence of love. I must be free (available) to leave my own self and selfish concerns to go out to you in a total readiness to listen and to be concerned (presence). While I am listening to you, you become the center of my world, the focus of my attention. My availability supposes that I am not so filled with my own emotions that I cannot leave them and listen with deep empathy to you and to your feelings. Wrenching free from the narcissism of self-preoccupation, especially when my emotions are painful, is difficult. However, it is a vital necessity for true listening and true dialogue. I cannot merely appear to be interested in you and what you are saying while I am in fact distracted by many other things. I must experience and convey the reality to you that my time, my mind, and my heart are yours. There is no one more important to me in this whole world right now than you.

If I have been successful in listening, I will convey to the speaker a reassuring: "I hear you!" And the speaker's reaction will be something like this: "Thank God! Someone finally knows what it is like to be me."

A good listener has an abiding respect for the inexhaustible mystery of the human person and its infinite varieties. Each experience in dialogue is a new discovery, an adventure into the previously unknown. The good listener does not have definite, prefabricated, inspected-and-approved expectations or anticipations concerning the person and revelation of the speaker. Having such expectations about what another can and cannot say gets a listener trapped in the "should-ought" box. And the one category that is not applicable to the riches of human emotions is that of should-ought.

Finally, a word of warning about "suppressive techniques." As everyone knows, communication can be either verbal or nonverbal. We can suppress intended communication in either way, and we probably will do so if we are threatened by dialogue. I can say something that is cynical or disruptive, or I can sidetrack you in subtle, nonverbal ways. I can yawn, look at my watch, tighten my jaws, narrow my eyes, raise my eyebrows, suddenly lean forward, change the volume or pitch of my voice. In any case, I will be communicating through "coded signals," and you will know that something is wrong. Those psychiatrists who use the traditional couch usually sit out of eye range of the patient so that none of their inadvertent reactions will be misinterpreted and cause the patient suddenly to clam up.

In evaluating our ability to listen in dialogue, we should check up on our possible use of these suppressive techniques. However, more reliable than our own recognition, and certainly more important to the success of our attempts at dialogue, would be the reaction of our partners in dialogue. We should sincerely ask them how often, by what mannerisms or "coded signals" they feel "put off." Remember: It's not what you say to people but what they hear that counts.

The Case of the Uncooperative Partner

The objection most often raised and the question most often asked in this whole area of dialogue is this: "What if I try but my partner simply will not cooperate—will not open up his or her feelings?" Many people claim to have this frustrating experience of unrequited self-disclosure. The fact is hard to ascertain, and the causes of unreturned self-disclosure are very difficult to diagnose.

There are, however, some presumptions and suggestions that a person in this position should investigate and evaluate with as much honesty as possible. First of all, I presume that all human beings want to be open, to be known and to be loved. Loneliness and alienation are painful conditions, and will be endured only when and if something worse is feared. If my partner in a relationship remains closed, he or she either has something to fear or thinks so. There is some reassurance that I have not been able to convey to him or her.

Most psychologists are of the opinion that if one of the parties in a love relationship really and truly opens up to the other as an act of loving self-disclosure, the other will soon reciprocate. The underlying reasoning of such reciprocity is: You have trusted me; I will trust you. Therefore, people with uncooperative partners might well ask themselves the following questions:

1 Am I truly opening myself to you as an act of love? Or have I been simply ventilating my own emotions, manipulating you?

2 Have I truly wanted unity, to know and to be known, or have my efforts of dialogue really been a pursuit of my own happiness and satisfaction?

3 Do I invite your openness only through my own openness, or do I pressure you? Do I poke with probing questions into areas that you have not voluntarily opened? Have I driven you into a defensive posture by my intrusive attacks on your privacy?

4 Do I have a sense that we are collaborators or competitors? Do I want you to be open more for your sake or for my own? If you did open up, would I feel that it was a victory for my perseverance or your victory over your own inhibitions?

5 What suppressive techniques might I be using without even knowing it? In general, do I look so depressed and fragile that you would not dare tell me the truth? Or do I look so domineering that you would not want to risk your secrets with me?

6 How have I received your attempts at openness in the past? Have I ever used your self-revelation to "hit back" in an argument?

7 Have I exposed my own needs, deficiencies, and incompleteness in such a way that you know that you do not have to fear me? Do you know of my need to know you, to share whatever you are and whatever is in you?

8 Am I, in general, the type who is always ready to give advice? Do I often feel that I know what is best for people even when they do not realize it themselves?

9 How do I speak of the confidence I have received from others? Do you see in me a judgmental, harsh, or condescending person? You may have seen the dried blood of others under my fingernails, and not wanted to risk your own tender flesh.

10 Am I too filled with my own emotions to be truly present and available to you and your feelings?

Negative Emotions

Obviously, the thorniest question about dialogue is that of negative emotions. What do I do when I feel hostile or even homicidal toward you? It happens, of course, in the best of families. There is a very definite risk and danger in telling you of my resentments, anger, bitterness, or hostility. Usually there is little or no risk in telling you of my grateful and loving feelings.

First of all, I feel sure that the growth of real love requires a commitment of total honesty between the two partners. They must agree from the outset that negative emotions will be just as welcome in dialogue as positive emotions. To see our way clear to this commitment of total honesty, we must face the fact that the only alternative to sharing in dialogue is somehow to "act out" these negative feelings. We can act them out on our selves (headaches, ulcers, and so forth) or on each other (in periods of silent pouting, in little games of spite, in the withholding of signs of affection, and the like). Or we can act them out on innocent bystanders (in yelling at the children, in being irritable with people at work or school, and so on).

Second, we must be convinced that the "friction" of negative emotions is not a bad sign at all, but rather a sign of health and vitality in a relationship. The absence of tensions or frictions is always a bad sign: The relationship itself is either dead or dying. Where there is life there is always some vital tension. Gibran says that we can easily forget those we have laughed with but we can never forget those with whom we have wept. It is also true that every relationship must have crises. They are really invitations to rise above those level plateaus, to go outside those "comfort zones" where we want to linger permanently. Crises are definitely invitations to growth, and those who courageously accept these invitations will find a new and fresh dimension in their love relationship.

More and more people today, educated by the world of advertisement that instant success and gratification are a law of life, are quitting. They are backing out of their love commitments without ever really challenging themselves and their coping abilities. Almost as sad are those who refuse to have a crisis because they refuse to endure the painful tensions that are part of a growing love relationship. They sadly settle for that twilight zone called "truce."

However, if you have really been buying what I have been selling, it will be clear that there is very little danger of disaster through the communication of negative emotions. I have been stating as a fact that no one causes our emotions and that all other judgments, accusations, and assignments of responsibility are alien to true dialogue. "So I'm angry," says the master of the dialogical art. "I'm angry because you were late. I well know that this anger is simply my reaction to the situation because of something in me. I also know that there are others, less scarred than I psychologically, who would react differently, maybe even sympathetically. But this is me at this moment in my life. I feel angry and even vindictive. I feel a

vengeful urge to put you through some kind of frustration or inconvenience, to make you wait on a lonely street corner for me. Of course, I won't do this. My emotions don't make my decisions for me. However, I just wanted you to know that this is how I feel. I've got anger and vengeance in me, I guess, and I want you to know that because I want you to know me."

A Healing Question

It is not strictly a part of dialogue, since it involves judgments and a decision, but it is an almost magical enabler and facilitator of dialogue. It is the simple request: "Will you forgive me?" The beginning of most human rifts that sabotage love and dialogue is what I have called a "wounded spirit." For example, I speak to you in a condescending manner or I say something to you that hurts. I may or may not realize the effects of my manner or words on you, but to a greater or lesser degree you are crushed. It may also happen that you do not tell me of your pain, but act it out on me. We can then easily be trapped in a getting-even game, a back and forth contest. When this begins, the lines of communication are down, the relationship is bleeding, and there is great need for healing. Our spirits have been wounded.

What I am suggesting here is that most ailing relationships can be restored to health almost miraculously by this simple

Ailing relationships can be restored to health
by this simple but sincere request:
"Will you forgive me?"

but sincere request: "Will you forgive me?" In asking the question, I am not assuming all blame. I am not deciding who was right and who was wrong. I am simply asking you to take me back into your love from which I have been separated. The acknowledged need for forgiveness is the most effective means of restoration for wounded spirits. No relationship should go on for very long without it.

The Emotional Reward
for Perseverance

We have said that any suggestion of competition undermines a love relationship and the practice of dialogue. The opposite and appropriate spirit is that of collaboration. It is a spirit that takes for granted that we are committed to each other in love, that we are willing to bear each other's burdens and share each other's joys. We have lost two I's to become one We. We will work at life's challenges together. We will succeed sometimes and sometimes we will fail, but we will be together. This sense of "togetherness" may well be the nicest and most sustaining awareness we will have. It is the joy of achieving together, of collaboration, of unity.

If self-appreciation and self-celebration are really the beginning of love and the fullness of life, we will achieve it together. You will look into my eyes and see there the great cause you have for self-celebration and I shall see my beauty, my value in your eyes. I want to be the first of the invited guests at your celebration-of-self party. And I want you to come to my party, because without you there never could have been such a party. Where there is unity like this, the butterfly of happiness cannot be far away.

If I had only a short time to live, I would immediately contact all the people I had ever really loved, and I'd make sure they knew I had really loved them. Then I would play all the records that meant the most to me, and I would sing all my favorite songs. And oh! I would dance. I would dance all night.

I would look at my blue skies and feel my warm sunshine. I would tell the moon and the stars how lovely and beautiful they are. I would say "good-bye" to all the little things I own—my clothes, my books, and my "stuff." Then I would thank God for the great gift of life, and die in his arms.

from a College Girl's Journal

CHAPTER SIX

Exercises in dialogue

When I began teaching in the "largest private university" in the state of Illinois, I sensed something of the blurring anonymity felt by many of the students: an absence of identity and personal recognition. I wondered what I would do to contribute to a solution of this problem, and decided that the very least would be to learn the first and last names of all my students. So I brought a Polaroid camera to the first class of each course, posed my students in groups of six, and had them write their names on the backs of the photos. On the night of the photographing I memorized all the names and faces.

For the first few years that I did this, I didn't realize how much more was possible. There were familiar names and faces out there, a spirit of friendly rapport, but I was not getting to know the persons under those names and behind those faces.

So I tried a new technique to supplement the pictures. I asked each student to write a "personal journal," listening to and recording his or her deepest feelings on twenty topics that I listed and somewhat detailed. It was a required assignment, but I gave my students the alternate option of a term paper of equivalent length. I wanted no part of confidence by coercion. As it turned out, almost all the students were either willing or eager to do the journal. Perhaps this willingness to take me into their confidence was a response to my own attempted openness. I had told them in class my own answers, my own feelings on the twenty topics. Transparency begets transparency. Openness is clearly contagious.

I am sure that the expected benefits accrued to the students. The unexpected was what happened to me. Suddenly persons emerged to go with those names and faces: troubled and tranquil, simple and complicated, mysterious and transparent, all at the same time. All that I had told my students about the transformation that results from peak experiences in communication was happening in me. I knew that I could never be the same again, that I could never think of "college kids" as kids again. So many of their lives had already borne adult burdens. Their emotions had been weather-beaten by raw and raging angers, suicidal depressions, but most of all by crippling fears that the "cool look" never allowed them to express.

Our self-image and esteem are influenced mostly by those who are closest to us. In the openness of their journals, I had come close to my students, had shared their secrets. Consequently, I knew that I must reflect back to them, in my acceptance and love, a reason to accept themselves with peace and joy, to find a real cause for celebration.

Of course, the personal journals occasioned many friendships among the students themselves. There was a spirit of trust and confidence among them, and inevitably among some an exchange of notebooks. One of the graduating seniors asked me if I was aware that the students in my class had come to know each other quickly and well. She said that many of them got together outside of class and some had formed lasting friendships. I am very grateful for this, and for whatever I can contribute to the lives and happiness of my students. My teaching is an important part of my "laboratory of life," where the theories and practices suggested in this book have been tested and found helpful, at least to me.

EXERCISE ONE

An Emotional Inventory

It might be good to start this exercise in dialogue by taking an inventory of our own experiences and various emotions. It is really very important to develop awareness with respect to our emotions. We can never really understand or share them until we begin to recognize them in our daily lives. Most people, when they first get into this "record and report" business of emotional awareness, do not realize the many shades and nuances of feeling of which we humans are capable.

The following is a partial (incomplete) list of emotions that the normal person feels from time to time. This exercise in recognition is designed to help us check up on our performance in recording and reporting our feelings. You are asked to do this by copying the number or writing out the name of the emotions listed below, taking ten at a time, and ten or more each day.

Use the following scale in rating your experience:

never 1

rarely 2

occasionally 3

often 4

very often 5

most of the time 6

almost constantly 7

After the name or number of each emotion, indicate with two other numbers from the scale above: (*a*) the frequency with which you experience this emotion, and (*b*) the frequency with which you report this experience to others. There may be a variation either way. For example, it could be that you feel "angry" *very often* (#5), but you express anger externally only *rarely* (#2). Or it might be that the variation will fall the other way. It may be that you feel "depressed" *occasionally* (#3), but you talk about it *very often* (#5).

Important. After you have completed this emotional inventory, show it to and talk it over with your partner in dialogue. This inventory is designed to be an aid to self-revelation and a springboard into further dialogue. When marking the questionnaire, you might well wonder about the precise meaning or description of many of the emotions listed. It is not really important what the dictionary says. The only important thing is your meaning and interpretation. Consequently, in the dialogue that will follow the filling out of this questionnaire, you will have to explain your meaning to your partner. You will have to explain what certain words mean to you. Feeling "angry" may mean something to one person and have another meaning for a second person. Consequently, explanation is essential. Such an exchange should invite each person to give a fuller description of the emotions that are felt and/or reported. Consult the suggestions, given in the previous chapter, on "how to speak" and "how to listen" in effective dialogue. Also try to discover the possible reasons why you feel this way, locating the ultimate cause within yourself and not blaming others. Also try to express the reasons why you do or do not report this feeling. Above all, concentrate on avoiding "shoulds" and "oughts." Remember that emotions do not have to be justified, explained, or excused. There is no such thing as a moral or immoral emotion, no such thing as a reasonable or unreasonable feeling.

Example: 1. accepted   5   2

Interpretation of example: I *very often* (#5) feel "accepted" but *rarely* (#2) report or express this feeling to others.

Emotional Checklist

1. accepted
2. accepting
3. affectionate
4. afraid
5. alarmed
6. alienated from others
7. alienated from self
8. angry
9. anxious
10. anxious to please others

11. apathetic
12. appreciated
13. attractive
14. awkward
15. beaten
16. beautiful
17. bewildered
18. brave
19. calm
20. cheated

21. closed
22. comfortable
23. committed
24. compassionate
25. competent
26. concerned for others
27. confident
28. confused

29. connected
30. contented

31. cop-out, like a
32. cowardly
33. creative
34. cruel
35. curious
36. cut off from others
37. defeated
38. dejected
39. dependent
40. depressed

41. deprived
42. deserving punishment
43. desperate
44. disappointed in myself
45. disappointed in others
46. dominated
47. domineering
48. eager to impress others
49. eager to please others
50. easily manipulated

51. easy going
52. embarrassed
53. envious
54. escape, desirous to
55. evasive

56. evil person, like an
57. excited
58. exhilarated
59. failure, like a
60. fatalistic

61. fearful
62. feminine
63. flirtatious
64. friendless
65. friendly
66. frigid
67. frustrated
68. generous
69. genuine
70. giddy

71. grateful
72. gratified by personal accomplishment
73. grudge-bearing
74. guilty
75. gutless
76. happy
77. hateable
78. hateful
79. homicidal
80. hopeful

81. hopeless
82. hostile
83. humorous
84. hurt

85. hurt by criticism
86. hyperactive
87. hypochondriacal (overly anxious about health)
88. hypocritical
89. ignored
90. immobilized

91. impatient
92. inadequate
93. incompetent
94. inconsistent
95. in control
96. indecisive
97. independent
98. inferior
99. inhibited
100. insanity, afraid of

101. insecure
102. insincere
103. involved
104. isolated
105. jealous

never	1
rarely	2
occasionally	3
often	4
very often	5
most of the time	6
almost constantly	7

106. judgmental
107. lonely
108. loser, like a
109. lovable
110. loved by another

111. loving of others
112. loyal
113. manipulated
114. manipulative of others
115. masculine
116. masked
117. masochistic
118. melancholy
119. misunderstood
120. needy

121. old beyond years
122. optimistic
123. out of contact with reality
124. out of control
125. overcontrolled
126. overlooked
127. oversexed
128. paranoid
129. passionate
130. peaceful

131. persecuted
132. pessimistic
133. phony

134. pity for others
135. played-out
136. pleased with others
137. pleased with self
138. possessive
139. poutful
140. preoccupied

141. prejudiced
142. pressured
143. protective of others
144. proud of others
145. proud of self
146. quiet
147. rejected
148. religious
149. remorseful
150. repelled by others

151. repulsive
152. restrained
153. rewarded
154. sad
155. sadistic
156. secure
157. seductive
158. self-complacent
159. self-pity, deserving of
160. self-reliant

161. sexually abnormal
162. sexually aroused

163. shallow
164. shy
165. silly
166. sincere
167. sinful
168. sluggish
169. soft
170. sorry for self

171. stubborn
172. stupid
173. suicidal
174. sunshiny
175. superior to others
176. supported
177. supportive
178. suspicious of others
179. sympathetic
180. tender

181. terrified
182. threatened
183. tolerant
184. torn
185. touchy
186. triumphant
187. two-faced
188. ugly
189. unable to communicate
190. unappreciated

191. uncertain of others

192. uncertain of self
193. understanding
194. ungifted
195. unresponsive
196. unrestrained
197. uptight
198. used by others
199. useless
200. victimized

201. vindictive
202. violent
203. weary of living
204. weepy
205. winner, like a
206. wishy-washy
207. youthful

never	1
rarely	2
occasionally	3
often	4
very often	5
most of the time	6
almost constantly	7

EXERCISE TWO

Writing and Exchanging "Personal Journals"

Most of us think we are better speakers than writers, which may be true since we do more speaking than writing. However, I would like to put in a strong word of encouragement for doing at least some writing, especially in the beginning and during the critical times of a love relationship.

First, there is less danger of suppressive techniques shutting off the free flow of communication. A human face has a thousand expressions, nine hundred of which can be construed as threatening. A blank page has only one look, which hasn't as yet frightened anyone.

Second, when you are going deep inside yourself, trying to find the right words to match the unrepeatable emotions of the moment, there will no doubt be prolonged, reflective pauses. People are generally not good at waiting. The page will wait. It has, unlike people, nothing else to do.

Last, there are many times when the dialogical mood just doesn't come upon the two partners simultaneously. Soon, promises and good intentions replace performance, and dialogue becomes one of those many things that you meant to keep in mind and get around to. Meanwhile, your love relationship gets duller and duller. With the use of notebook journals, each of the dialoguing partners can pick the most opportune time and write for as long or as little as he or she pleases.

Begun in Spain, Marriage Encounter is a movement that promotes dialogue and expression of feelings by married couples. It has been welcomed in the United States by

thousands of couples who have benefited from its encouragement in these communication areas of the love relationship.
Most participants in the Marriage Encounter movement have
found this practice invaluable and irreplaceable. Each of the
partners writes every day for ten minutes in a journal, and
then ten minutes are spent in exchanging journals and
dialoguing on what has been written. Most Encounter couples
testify that this habit of ten/ten guarantees a progressive
depth of understanding, acceptance, and love. The love and
happiness that these couples exude seem to substantiate their
testimony. I am sure that by and large the many couples I
have known from the Marriage Encounter movement represent the happiest marriages and are the happiest people I
know.

Marriage Encounter is for the married, but you don't have
to be married to experience the value of dialogue. So find
yourself a notebook and pen. Begin now with your partner
in dialogue to discover for yourselves what this kind of sharing
can mean to a love relationship. On the following pages you
will find forty suggested entry topics. It is recommended that
you take one each day. Read over the questions given there.
Then listen to your own answers and emotional reactions. Try
to verbalize these as vividly as possible in your journal.

Some of the suggested lines of reflection and listening under
the heading of each entry topic may seem to be directed
more to the mind than to the recapturing of emotions. Please
remember, however, that it is the emotional content in your
answer that will be unique to you. It is through the
communication of your emotions or feelings that you will
most effectively be communicating yourself to your partner
in dialogue. Finally, you may well find yourself with ambivalent
emotions with regard to the same object or person. Each of
us is a unique blend of such disparate, ambivalent emotions.

We have love and resentment, certainty and doubt, joy and sadness, hope and despair arising in us simultaneously. In trying to verbalize your feelings in these journal entries, be ready to welcome the emergence of such ambivalent feelings about one and the same topic.

Entry Topics

1   Messages on Your Parent Tapes

What messages, recorded in you during childhood, most influence your present attitudes and behavior? You need not remember any special words or formal statements made to you. Example is more eloquent than words. You will know which messages are most operative and influential from the recurring emotional patterns, drives, and inhibitions that you are currently experiencing. What did your parents (and other early influences) tell you about (1) you and your worth, (2) other people (Can they be trusted? Are they good? Do you have to be careful?), (3) life (What is life for? Is it to win something? To work hard? To save and be safe?)? After you have recorded these messages, listen to and report your own emotional reaction. Do you feel sympathy, resentment, pity, or what toward your parents and others from whom you heard these messages?

2   My Child

The child in us is our recorded and stored-up emotional response to the events of the first five years of life. Since most of these responses from ages one to five are on the feeling level, the child in us is our emotional storehouse, the part of us where all our emotions reside, from joy to despair. Others can stimulate but not cause these emotions to gush forth. Listen now to your child and try to describe as vividly as you can the predominant emotions of your child. These accumulated emotions, stored up in your first five years, will be recognized by the more consistent emotional reaction patterns of your whole life since. For example, does your child feel rejected, lonely, inferior, "picked on," overlooked? Is your child ever joyful, exuberant, creative, whimsical, free enough to do harmlessly "crazy" things? Has your child got a lot of anger stored up inside? Does he or she feel mostly secure or insecure, comfortable or uncomfortable?

3 The Past

Do you live with warm memories of your past? Or do you fear the past, worrying that it will someday return with all its ghosts and skeletons to haunt you? Does the remembrance of past failures or guilt tug at the masks of confidence you are trying to wear now? Does your ethnic background or the fact that you were rich, poor, or middle-class stir feelings in you now? How would you feel about going back to your old neighborhood, or seeing your grade or high school friends now? Do you experience any desire to show them what you have become? Do you enjoy talking over (sharing) your past with those who are closest to you now, or are you reluctant to do so? Do you like to resurrect your past, or would you rather bury it? All things considered, when you think about your past, do you feel privileged or cheated, grateful or resentful?

4 Yourself in Two Adjectives

If you were asked "Who are you?" and you had to respond by giving two descriptive adjectives rather than your name, which two adjectives would you pick? Which two adjectives best "capture" the real you and the dominant traits of your personality? After you pick two such adjectives that would best characterize you at this time in your life, describe in vivid detail what each adjective means to you. (You also might find it interesting to select two adjectives that you feel best describe your partner in dialogue and to have your partner choose two adjectives that would best portray you. It is stimulating, after we have looked at and listened to ourselves, to know how others see and hear us.)

5 Ten-Statement Autobiography

What are the ten most essential things anyone would have to know about you in order to understand in depth the real you? These statements should not include any obvious external facts that are visible to all who know you. Rather, they should reveal the person under all the costumes and roles, your deepest reality as opposed to your surface appearance. For example, "I have always been afraid of the opposite sex . . . The turning point of my whole life was my mother's death . . ." While each sentence should express a clear and complete meaning in itself, it is obvious that this meaning will have to be filled out in the dialogue that takes place at the time notebooks are exchanged.

6 Your Obituary

We usually say all our nice things about people only after they are dead. We try never to say nice things about ourselves, at least not in an obvious way. In your own "advance obituary" try to work up the nerve to verbalize all that is good, decent, and lovable in yourself. If you were to die at this point in your life, how would you summarize your life and your person? Do not use the usual "who—what—where—when" format. Try rather to describe who you really were, your greatest achievement, your most consistent virtue. Include the most unusual thing about yourself, your most endearing quality, your greatest ability, and the thing for which you will always be remembered. Finally, at the end of your obituary compose an epitaph to be inscribed on your tombstone which would best summarize everything. "Here lies a . . ."

7 *Greatest Emotional Need*

In the development of human personality, deprivation of needs, especially early in life, can leave a void that we try for the rest of our lives to fill. In one sense everyone could honestly say that his or her greatest emotional need is the love of another person. However, love asks: "What do you need me to do, to be for you?" Of course, our needs change from day to day, but what is the general answer you would give to someone who came to you in an act of love, asking: "What do you need me to do, to be for you?"

8 *Three Experiences of Humiliation*

Relate in your journal three experiences or incidents—one from childhood, one from adolescence, and one from your adult life—in which you felt crushed, hurt, humiliated. Describe in detail the incident itself but especially your feelings at that time. (Sharing such experiences has an unbelievably "opening" effect on partners in dialogue. Sharing old hurts and needs somehow removes the veils of our sham and pretended self-sufficiency. It is an eloquent way of saying: "You don't have to be afraid of me. The little kid who stood there alone in the school yard crying is still inside me. I need you." Nothing is more reassuring to the hesitant, fearful partner in dialogue.)

9 *Identity Niche*

Each of us wants to be recognized as an individual, to find a sense of unique personal worth. Early in life we pick an "identity niche," usually a role that would be noticed and appreciated by our parents. If a given role has already been chosen by an older brother or sister, we usually look for a different niche. For example, if my older sister is the "brain," and my brother is the "brawn," I will have to specialize in something else. I may choose to be "the funny one" or the "religious" child. In the event that I feel I have no quality or ability to individuate me, I may choose the course of what is called negative identity, the role of "troublemaker." I will get my recognition as "disturber of the peace." Of course, these identities change during life, but it is important to recognize and to share our current inclination. Admirable as an identity may be in itself, it is always an obstacle to complete communication. For example, if my identity is that of being a "helper," I will derive my sense of personal worth and emotional support from this identity. Consequently, I will "edit" my communication so that somehow I will always stay in the role of helper to helped. I will not tell you of my needs or ask for your help because that would be a reversal of roles. It would endanger my identity and threaten my sense of personal worth. What is your identity niche? As a consequence of this chosen niche, what do you find most difficult to share?

10   Being Loved

If someone of unquestionable sincerity and sound judgment were to say to you, "I love you," how would you react interiorly? Are you able to accept love happily? Can you surrender to the joy of being loved without suspicion of mistaken identity or fear of later rejection? Do you feel free about being yourself with someone who loves you, or are you extra careful not to disillusion that person and lose his or her love?

11   *Strongest Recent Emotion*

In the past six months or year of your life, what was your deepest and strongest emotion? If there were several, just pick one. Record something of the occasion and circumstances of stimulation but mostly describe the feeling as vividly as you can. It will invite your partner in dialogue to experience it with you.

12   *Self-knowledge*

How do you feel about knowing yourself? Do you like to take psychological tests, to have your handwriting analyzed? How would you feel if a psychiatrist offered to inject you with a "truth serum" and tape-record your answers to searching questions about yourself, your true feelings, motives, and desires? Do you have ambivalent emotions in this matter, partly curious and partly fearful of what you might find in yourself?

13   *Feelings about Self*

On a scale from 1 (lowest) to 10 (highest), rating human beings as you know them, where would you rate yourself? To call up your truest and most habitual feelings about yourself, it may help to close your eyes for a minute, and to see yourself coming out of a door, meeting there with a group of others and relating to them. Watch and listen to yourself. Watch your typical reaction when a favor is asked of you, when a compliment is paid to you, when you are criticized, when the group laughs at you. Did you like or dislike yourself as you watched and listened? How did you seem to compare with the others? Did you feel sorry for yourself in some ways? Are there any questions you would like to ask yourself? Would you like yourself for a friend? Did you seem to be understood or misunderstood by others, liked or disliked by them? After you have isolated your feelings about yourself, record your emotional reaction to these feelings. For example, "I liked myself but feel embarrassed to acknowledge this." Or, "I disliked myself and it makes me feel very discouraged."

14 Costume

It has been said that every costume makes a statement. We are saying something and revealing something about ourselves by the colors and styles of the clothes we choose. What is your statement? Do you adopt the latest fashions, the "in" type clothes because you feel obliged to conform, or is it a matter of pure enjoyment for you? Do you choose and wear your kind of clothes more to please yourself, someone else, or others in general? Do you tend to be more conservative or "mod"? Are clothes to you more functional or decorative? Would you like others to turn and look at you because of your attractive clothes, or would you feel self-conscious? In general, what feelings surface in you when you think about clothes and about what you are saying by the way you dress?

15 Body

When you last stood naked before a full-length mirror, what were your reactions? Were you pleased or embarrassed at the sight of your body? Is the health of your body more important to you than its appearance? Would you go on a "crash diet,"

Every costume makes a statement.
We are saying something about ourselves
by the colors and styles of clothes we choose.

which could possibly be harmful to your health, if you knew it would greatly improve your appearance? What do you feel when you think that someone is looking at your body? Which of your physical features do you like best? Least? In what part or organ of your body are you most prone to sickness. What is your usual emotional reaction to photos of yourself? What are your feelings about "touching"? Do you feel good or uneasy to be touched? Are you a "touching" type person? If so, what do you think you are trying to say in your touches?

16 Sexuality

Are you comfortable or uncomfortable with the fact that you are a sexual being? What were your feelings when you saw that this was the next entry topic of your journal? Are you "troubled" by sexual feelings and fantasies, or can you accept them as a wholesome, natural, and good part of your human nature? What does it mean to you emotionally to be a woman—a man? Do you feel secure in your femininity— masculinity? Or do you feel a need to "prove yourself"? Does your notion of sexuality pertain to something you *do* or to something you *are?* In your own mind and emotions, are love, personhood, and sexuality inseparable?

17 Weakness

To what extent are you comfortable with your human condition of weakness? To what extent do you feel the urge to rationalize and justify your mistakes? Are you embarrassed or angered to be caught in some form of failure? How do you feel about the undeniable weaknesses of your past life? Are you afraid of future failures? Does reappearance of weakness surprise you? Which is harder for you to accept in yourself—psychological weaknesses (fears, complexes) or moral weaknesses (sins)? Which specific weakness—for example, shyness, explosions of temper, overeating, excessive drinking—causes you the most emotional discomfort? Do you find it easier to forgive weakness in others or in yourself?

18   One Change in Self

In your interaction with others, of which limitation in yourself are you most conscious? What is the greatest obstacle, as you see yourself, to self-acceptance, self-esteem, and self-celebration? What limitation in yourself do you make the greatest effort to conceal from others? Do you feel that the one change you would most like to make in yourself is the same as that which might be preferred by those closest to you? What feelings arise in you when you see in yourself the quality or limitation you would like to change? Do you have a sense of failure about not yet accomplishing this change? What feelings are an obstacle to making this change?

19   Possessions

When you read the word *possessions,* did you first think about material things or personal qualities and abilities? In terms of your emotional reactions, are your riches inside you or outside? Of all your material possessions, to which do you feel most strongly attached? In case of a fire in your house, what is the one thing you would be sure to take with you? Describe your feelings about this object and try to explain why you feel so strongly about it. Do you ever feel that your material possessions are construed by you as an extension of yourself, so that what you are is somehow reinforced by what you have? How do you feel about showing people through your home or exhibiting your possessions? Do you ever feel a value conflict between persons and things? When you are introduced to people considerably wealthier than you, are your emotional reactions different than when you are meeting people at your own economic level or less well off than you? Which of your personal abilities do you most rely on, take greatest pleasure in, and would hate most to lose?

20 *Mine and/or Thine*

(This question pertains to the mutual attitudes of the chosen partners in dialogue.) Are most of my feelings about our relative abilities emotions of competition or collaboration? Do I have a feeling of one-upmanship? Do I feel involved in a contest or a unification of talents? Is it more important to me that I emerge as superior or that we accomplish together? Do we concede "areas of competence" to each other, but compete in other areas? After we have disagreed on some matter, what are my feelings when it turns out that I have been right? When you have been right? Do I truly rejoice in your successes, or are there also emotions of envy and fear that your successes might overshadow my own? Does my "sex" and yours affect these feelings of competition or collaboration?

21 *Sources of Greatest Satisfaction*

Enjoyment is certainly an essential part of the fullness of life. Each person draws enjoyment, however, from his or her own special sources: from wandering through a forest, reading a book, playing a sport or a musical instrument, conversing with a friend, and so on. There is a special reward of peace at the end of a "perfect day," filled with these special sources of gratification. Describe your idea of a perfect day and the feelings special to such a day. Is the accomplishment of a task or job more satisfying to you than the accomplishment of a deep sharing with another person? Is your perfect day filled mostly with things, ideas, or persons?

22 Fundamental Attitude toward Others

What are your anticipations in first meeting people? Do you expect to like everyone until contrary evidence excludes some? Or do you expect to like only the very few who can survive your cautious scrutiny? Are you guided more by your heart or by your head in relating to people? Describe how you feel upon entering a room full of strangers. Are you initially enthusiastic about people, but feel hurt and disappointed when they prove to have real faults and limitations? Or are you rather skeptical at first and grow only gradually in your appreciation of others? Whichever way you are, how do you feel about being that way?

23 Intimacy

Are you comfortable or uncomfortable at the prospect of being very close to another, knowing and being known as completely as possible? Intimacy has frightening aspects for everyone. What would you fear most about intimacy? Do you find intimacy easier with people to whom you are related (family) or with friends? How important are friends to you? If you had to move from your present location, how deeply would you feel the loss of their immediate presence? Are you more inclined to express your love for others by deep personal sharing and confiding or by doing things for them? Have you made a considerable emotional investment in your friends? How do you feel about your own present attitudes toward and accomplishments of human closeness? If you had to call someone in the middle of the night in an emergency, who would you call and why?

24 Responsibility

Do you feel an emotional compulsion to help others, even beyond reasonable limits? Do your emotions of responsibility fall in line with your prudent judgment of your capacities? Do you feel responsible for larger social problems such as city ghettos, increased crime, health care, mental illness? Do you feel an obligation to get involved politically? Do you ever feel guilty for failure to become more involved? Do you ever feel powerless and consequently relieved of responsibility? Do many or few people confide their problems to you? How do you interpret this? What does this say to you about you? What feelings does this stimulate in you?

25 Sources of Emotional Support

Studies show that people with a greater sense of responsibility have a correspondingly greater need for emotional support from others, but at the same time such people find it harder to accept such support. Classify and describe yourself and your feelings and inclinations in the light of this statement.

26 Needing Others

Is it emotionally satisfying or humbling for you to need others, to have to seek their help? When helped, do you feel an urge to repay them, to balance the scales as soon as possible? Do you emotionally grasp the truth that letting others help you is a way of loving them? Are there special areas of need in which you find it emotionally difficult to ask for or accept help? Can you easily talk over your problems with another? Can you ask for and accept help in the form of listening?

27 Privacy

Are there areas of your life around which you prefer a fence? When others question you about your whereabouts, activities, and so on, do you feel as though you are being "frisked," invaded, or somehow threatened? Do you ever feel a psychological claustrophobia, closed in by and overexposed to people? Do you have special techniques to defend your privacy, for example, humor, changing the subject, giving vague and distracting responses? What are your motives for wanting privacy? Is it a learned habit from family background, or guilt feelings, or perhaps a fear of vulnerability as a result of being known?

28 Dialogue

Do most of your emotions move you toward or away from dialogue? What do you have that might be threatened by dialogue? What do you have to lose? Does dialogue for you represent a special risk? What are your feelings of need for dialogue? What emotional needs are you aware of that might be fulfilled in dialogue? To what extent might the self-discipline required for daily dialogue affect your evaluation of such a dialogue? How would you compare your attitude toward dialogue with that of your partner? Do any special emotions result from this comparison?

29 Commitments

True love is a decision-commitment to the satisfaction, security, and development of another. Once you have committed yourself, the big question is: Are you going to be faithful because you *have to* or because you *want to?* How do you feel about the commitments you have already made? Is there more of a joyless "have to" or an eager "want to"? How do you feel when you come to the brink of a new, possible commitment? Are you frightened at the thought of irrevocability, of getting into something and not being able to get out of it? Do your commitments ever result in the "quicksand" feeling? When things are going poorly in a relationship, do you feel discouraged and impelled to back out? Or are you rather determined and stimulated by the challenge? Do you ever feel afraid that somewhere in your life, through your commitments, you got off the right track and what has followed has all been a mistake?

30 Authority Figures

Wherever we are, no matter how old we are, there are always authority figures: the teacher demanding homework, the boss checking up on our work, the policeman telling us to stop our cars. There are basically two general reactions to authority figures of serious emotional import. The first is conformity—wanting to please those in authority. Conformists are afraid of conflict, dislike trouble. They prefer law and order, are careful to use zip codes, and mail their Christmas cards early. There is an emotion of satisfaction that comes to them in always doing the "right thing." The other basic reaction is rebellion. Any symbols of authority are signals to the rebels' adrenalin. Those in authority are always wrong: the president, the pope, the mayor, the school principal. All of them are bad news. Bosses are unreasonable and teachers are unfair. The Child in the conformist is predominantly docile, looking for okayness and approval. The Child in the rebel is angry, telling every authority figure: "You're not OK. You hurt me, and it's gonna cost you!" Of course, a thousand variations of these two people and positions are possible. Listen to and describe the pattern of your emotional reactions to authority figures.

Once you have committed yourself,
the big question is:
Are you going to be faithful
because you have to or because you want to?

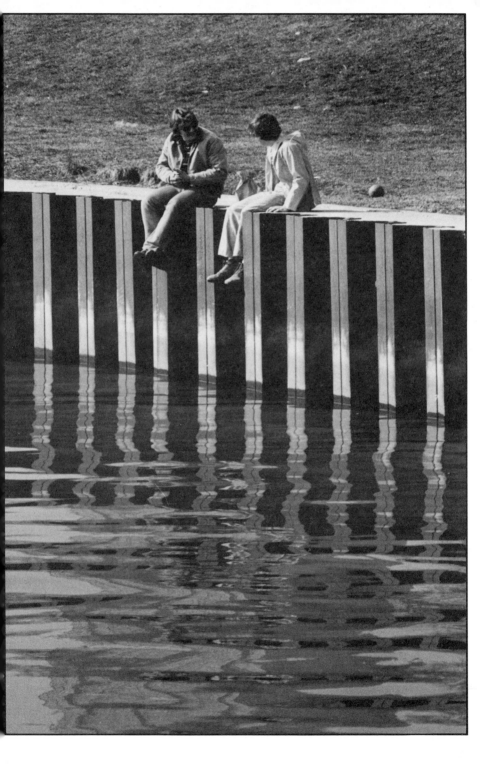

31 Hardest Emotion to Share

Sometimes we allow ourselves to experience emotions (we do not repress them), but we cannot admit or express these feelings to others. This inhibition possibly arises from our programming, some value conflict or a fear that others would not understand. Perhaps our society or peer group has quarantined certain emotions out of sight, such as feeling sorry for oneself or jealousy. Men are very often unable to admit fear or express tenderness. Women are often reluctant to report hostility or envy. Describe the one emotion you find most difficult to admit and express, and as far as you can locate them, the reasons for this difficulty. For example, "I have great difficulty admitting fear because my father told me a real man is never afraid."

32 God

What emotions does the thought of "God" stimulate in you? In general, do you feel like a child in the lap of your father, a student in a classroom, a person in debt dealing with your creditor, a slave standing before your master? What does the thought of God do to you? Affirm? Reprehend? Frighten? Support? Console? Free? Inhibit? If God had a face, describe the look God would most probably give you and then verbalize what that look is telling you. Have you ever felt angry at God—a perfectly legitimate emotion—for not granting a favor or for taking away a loved one in death? Do you ever feel estranged, separated, distant from God? What is your emotional reaction to theological God talk? Could this reaction reflect some other deeper feelings in you? What were your feelings at the time in your life when God seemed most "real" to you?

33 *Parents*

Most people have a whole range of emotions stored up inside
them toward each of their parents, from tender affection to
bitter resentment. However, this is an area in which we have
all received carefully supervised psychological programming.
Our attitudes have been carefully shaped by our parents and
others. Consequently, we tend to edit our feelings toward our
mothers and fathers, especially if the parent in question is
deceased. Describe here your most basic emotional reactions
to each of your parents. Remember that negative emotions
are no indictment of your parents. It isn't what they said but
only what you heard that has resulted in your feelings. Is/was
either of your parents a friend and confidant as well as a parent
to you? What feelings were stimulated by the last question
and your answer to it?

34 *Family*

Try to verbalize the most fundamental message you have heard
from your immediate family about yourself and your relationship with the members of your family. Is it a message of
acceptance or mere toleration, affection or disaffection, desire
to be closer or more distant, of admiration or disapproval?
Remember again, you are verbalizing only what you have
heard. For this you don't need a reason, proof, or excuse. This
is what you have heard and these are your consequent feelings.
After verbalizing your family's reactions and message to you,
try to verbalize your feelings and your message to your family
in the same way.

35 *Goals*

No life is complete without a reason or motive, something
or someone to love and to work for. What are your life goals
and what is your life task as you see them right now? Have you

made a deep emotional investment in these goals, or are they showpieces, more a matter of lip service than life-style? On your emotional scales, what are the five things that are most important and most worth working for in life? Does your main occupation, the thing at which you spend most of your time and energy, reflect your priorities in life? Do you spend most of your time and energy on something you feel is important and valuable? How do you feel about this?

36 Life Cycles

Life is a death-resurrection cycle. In every moment there is a *death,* a leaving what has been, and a *birth,* a stepping into what is and will be. We must leave things behind: the warmth of our mothers' wombs, privileged infant status, childhood toys, the irresponsible joys of youth, the protection of family and dependent status, jobs, locations, and so on. And in the end, we gradually lose our physical strength, our teeth, hearing, and vision. There is a constant emotional tension in most people between wanting to go back and reclaim what has been and an eagerness to embrace the new. Describe your feelings, sadnesses, fears, hopes, anticipations. In going through these inevitable stages, do you feel mostly brave or afraid, mostly glad or sad? Do you yearn for "the good old days," or do your emotions believe that the best is yet to come?

37 The Future

Describe your predominant emotional reaction to your anticipated future. Are you eager for the future or afraid of the uncertainties? Do you dread the things that you see as inevitable? Calculate as best you can where you will be and what you will be doing in five years. In ten years. Is the prospect frightening, boring, dreadful, or delightful? What do you feel about who will decide your future? Do you have a feeling of being in control of your life? Do you anticipate that you will determine your future? Or do you have fatalistic-type feelings that the "breaks" (good and bad) will largely decide your fate and your future?

38 Growing Old

What do you feel when someone asks you how old you are? What age would you like to be? Someone has said that "the pessimist sees the difficulty in every opportunity; the optimist sees the opportunity in every difficulty." Does growing old seem like all difficulty to you, or are there feelings of opportunity that arise in you? Robert Browning wrote: "Grow old along with me!/The best is yet to be,/The last of life, for which the first was made." What feelings do these lines stir in you? When you see aged people, what are your feelings for them? What feelings do they stimulate in you about the anticipation of being aged yourself?

39 Suffering and Pain

Most people are better at enduring one form of suffering or pain than another. What forms of suffering or pain are most difficult for you? Why? Is there any specific suffering or pain for which you have a particular dread or even phobia? From what do you suffer most frequently in your life? Intellectually we know that suffering can be very profitable, and we may even know that past sufferings have brought great blessings. Do you ever have grateful, welcoming feelings in the midst of suffering? If someone could offer you a pill that would have no other effect but the elimination of suffering for the rest of your life, would you take it? Why or why not? Would you give such a pill to those you love? Do you feel an inner urgency to eliminate all suffering in your own life, and in the lives of those you love? Do you often have feelings of satisfaction when another person is struggling and you have hopes that he or she will emerge a better person? What suffering or pain in the past year of your life affected you most deeply?

40 Death

In your imagination see yourself on your deathbed. The doctor says that it will be only a matter of hours now. How would you feel? Describe whatever fears, regrets, satisfactions, peace, panic, or hopes might come to you. If you were completely conscious and aware, what would you do with those last hours of life? In a separate exercise of imagination, try to visualize yourself in a doctor's office, getting the diagnosis of terminal illness, with months or maybe even a year or two to live. Describe your anticipated emotional reaction. It has been said that we all deny our mortality, that we pretend we are not going to die. Do you repress or look away from the thought of dying? Do you think rarely, sometimes, or often of your own dying? What were your deepest emotions when you most recently lost a loved one in death? Do you find the confrontation with death at "wakes" difficult? What bothers you most? Do you feel you have to or would like to say something to the bereaved family to help take the "sting" out of death? Would you emotionally rather have the one you love most in this world die before you or follow you in death? Does the thought of or belief in an afterlife actively influence your emotional reactions to dying?

EXERCISE THREE
Topics for the Daily Ten/Ten

As a final incentive for continued dialogue I would like to leave you with a list of topics for daily dialogue. I think of the forty entry topics already given as the "essential material" of self-revelation. In a continued dialogue they should be reviewed every year, since emotional reactions and patterns change as we reshuffle our priorities and review our prejudices. However, life is filled with many other wonderful, humorous, and traumatic moments. The following questions are meant to capture some of them, but the list could never be completed. You will think of many more. Remember that anything that causes emotional reactions is a good topic for dialogue. As you get more and more in touch with your emotions, your personal list of such topics will fill many notebooks. For now, look through these topics and choose those that resonate in you emotionally. Let each partner in dialogue reflect and write for ten minutes, and then spend ten minutes sharing and dialoguing on what you have written.

How Do I Feel When—

. . . you surprise me with something nice?
. . . you seem to appreciate me?
. . . you laugh at my jokes?
. . . I think of how our children are turning out?
. . . I think that you are not recognizing my needs?
. . . I make a mistake and you point it out?
. . . you are holding me in your arms?
. . . our routines or different interests separate us?
. . . I am late and you have to wait for me?
. . . you are late and I have to wait for you?

. . . you have a strong interest that I cannot share?

. . . I try to convince you of something and you can't accept it?

. . . you seem to be rejecting my feelings?

. . . you praise or compliment me?

. . . I am confronted with or think of that which I fear most?

. . . I think that you are judging me?

. . . you become violently angry with me?

. . . I think of praying with you?

. . . you make a sacrifice for me?

. . . others notice our closeness?

. . . we appear as a partnership, not as individuals only?

. . . I reflect that you love me?

. . . you seem annoyed with me?

. . . I have the opportunity to be alone, enjoy some solitude?

. . . we have been separated for a long time?

. . . I reflect that we are growing in mutual knowledge?

. . . we are holding hands?

. . . we are making plans together?

. . . I am buying you a gift?

. . . I think you are taking a superior role in our dialogues and discussions?

. . . I do not seem able to reach you?

. . . you frown at me?

. . . you are being too hard on yourself?

. . . you smile at me?

. . . you reach out to touch me?

. . . I reach out to touch you?

. . . you interrupt me in conversation?

. . . we are in some form of competition, like cards or an athletic contest?

. . . you say "no" to one of my requests?

. . . I think I have hurt your feelings?

. . . you apologize to me?

. . . we can spend a quiet evening together?

. . . you help me locate my feelings?

. . . I hear from others that you have bragged about me?

. . . I hear from others that you have complained about me?

. . . some other interest seems more important to you than I do?

. . . you seem to be holding something back from me?

. . . I am holding something back from you?

. . . you look at other women (men) with obvious interest?

. . . others look at you with obvious interest?

. . . you cry?

. . . you are sick?

. . . I think about your death, and what life will be without you?

. . . we hear "our song"?

. . . you ask me to dance with you?

. . . you ask me to help you?

. . . I think you don't believe me?

. . . I have to apologize to you?

Conclusion

Dialogue is to love what blood is to the body. When the flow of blood stops, the body dies. When dialogue stops, love dies and resentment and hatred are born. But dialogue can restore a dead relationship. Indeed this is the miracle of dialogue.

Reuel Howe, *The Miracle of Dialogue*

There are no winners and losers in dialogue, only winners. Neither partner is ever required to give up or to give in but only to give, to give of the self. In dialogue we can never end up with less than we were but only more. To live in dialogue with another is to live twice. Joys are doubled by exchange and burdens are cut in half by sharing.

The listening and the speaking of dialogue, each with its own particular set of consequences, are each directed to the other. Dialogue is essentially other-centered. Dialogue is essentially an act of the purest love and the secret of staying in love.